Efficient and Parallel Python Programming

: A Practical Handbook for Mastering Concurrent Development to Build Scalable, Responsive, and High-Performance Applications

Matthew D.Passmore

Table Of Content

Part 1: Foundations of Concurrent and Parallel Programming

Chapter 1
Introduction: The Need for Speed and Scalability

In today's data-driven world, applications are constantly pushed to their limits. We expect instant results, seamless handling of large datasets, and the ability to adapt to growing user demands. This is where the concepts of speed and scalability become paramount.

Limitations of Sequential Programming:

Traditional sequential programming, where tasks are executed one after another, often struggles to meet these demands. Processing large datasets or performing complex calculations can lead to slow response times and frustration for users. Additionally, sequential programs are limited in their ability to handle concurrent requests efficiently.

Introducing Concurrency and Parallelism:

This is where concurrent and parallel programming come into play. Concurrency allows multiple tasks to appear to be running simultaneously, even on a single processor. This can be achieved through techniques like multithreading, where different parts of a program run concurrently within the same process.

Parallelism, on the other hand, leverages multiple processors or cores to execute tasks truly simultaneously. By distributing the workload across multiple processing units, we can achieve significant speedups compared to sequential execution.

Benefits of Efficient and Parallel Programming:

Mastering efficient and parallel programming techniques offers several key benefits:

Improved Application Performance: By utilizing concurrency and parallelism, applications can handle complex tasks and large datasets much faster, leading to a smoother user experience.

Enhanced Scalability: Parallel programming allows applications to scale efficiently by adding more processing power. This is crucial for handling growing user loads and data volumes.

Increased Responsiveness: By utilizing techniques like asynchronous programming, applications can remain responsive even when handling multiple requests or I/O operations simultaneously. This leads to a more user-friendly experience.

The Road Ahead:

This book will delve deep into the world of concurrent and parallel programming in Python. We'll explore the fundamental concepts, practical techniques using libraries like threading, multiprocessing, and asyncio, and strategies for optimizing code and building scalable applications. By the end, you'll be equipped to unlock the true potential of Python for building high-performance, responsive, and future-proof applications.

1.1 Limitations of Sequential Programming

While sequential programming has been the foundation of software development for decades, it faces significant challenges in today's demanding computing environment. Here's a closer look at its limitations:

Slow execution for complex tasks: Sequential programs process instructions one after another. This linear approach can be incredibly slow for computationally intensive tasks or those involving large datasets. Imagine a program analyzing millions of data points; each point needs to be processed sequentially, leading to lengthy execution times.

Poor utilization of multi-core processors: Modern computers often have multiple cores or processors that can handle tasks simultaneously. However, sequential programs are limited to using a single core at a time, leaving the remaining processing power unused. This underutilization translates to wasted potential for faster execution.

Inability to handle concurrent requests efficiently: In today's world, applications often handle multiple user requests concurrently. Sequential programs struggle to manage these requests effectively. Each request needs to wait for the previous one to finish before it can be processed, leading to delays and a sluggish user experience.

Limited responsiveness for I/O-bound tasks: Many applications involve interactions with external resources like databases or network connections. These interactions can be slow, and a sequential program has to wait for each I/O operation to complete before moving on. This waiting time can lead to a feeling of unresponsiveness for users interacting with the application.

In essence, sequential programming works well for simple tasks but struggles to keep up with the demands of modern applications that require speed, scalability, and the ability to handle multiple requests simultaneously.

1.2 Concurrency vs Parallelism: Understanding the Differences

The terms concurrency and parallelism are often used interchangeably, but there's a subtle yet crucial distinction between them. Both concepts aim to improve program performance by managing multiple tasks, but they differ in how those tasks are actually executed.

Concurrency: The Illusion of Simultaneity

Concurrency focuses on the management of multiple tasks that appear to be running at the same time. This "appearance" is achieved through a technique called context switching. The operating system rapidly switches between different tasks, giving the illusion that they are executing simultaneously.

Here's an analogy: Imagine a chef preparing a multi-course meal. While some ingredients are simmering, the chef can chop vegetables for another course. Concurrency is like this chef – efficiently managing multiple tasks, but only dealing with one active task at a time.

Key points about concurrency:

Can be achieved on a single CPU using context switching. Useful for I/O bound tasks where the program spends time waiting for external resources. Requires careful synchronization to avoid race conditions (where multiple tasks access shared data inconsistently).

Parallelism: True Simultaneous Execution

Parallelism, on the other hand, refers to the actual execution of multiple tasks simultaneously. This is achieved by utilizing multiple processing units (cores) within a CPU or even across multiple CPUs in a distributed system.

Imagine the same chef scenario, but with two chefs working together. One can handle the simmering ingredients, while the other chops vegetables. This is parallelism – two tasks genuinely happening at the same time.

Key points about parallelism:

Requires multiple processing cores or CPUs to achieve true simultaneous execution.
Ideal for CPU-bound tasks where most of the program's time is spent on calculations.
Communication and coordination between parallel tasks might be needed.

Choosing Between Concurrency and Parallelism:

The choice between concurrency and parallelism depends on the nature of your program's tasks.

If your program involves a lot of waiting for external resources (like I/O operations), concurrency can be a good choice to keep things moving.

If your program is computationally intensive and can be broken down into independent tasks, parallelism is the way to go for significant speedups.

In essence, concurrency provides the illusion of doing many things at once on a single CPU, while parallelism is the real deal, leveraging multiple processors to achieve true simultaneous execution. Understanding these distinctions is crucial for writing efficient and scalable programs in Python.

1.3 Benefits of Efficient and Parallel Programming

In today's data-driven world, applications are constantly bombarded with demands for speed, responsiveness, and the ability to handle ever-growing volumes of data. Traditional sequential programming methodologies often fall short in these areas. This is where efficient and parallel programming techniques come to the rescue, offering a multitude of benefits for modern applications.

1. Enhanced Performance:

Faster execution of complex tasks: By leveraging concurrency and parallelism, applications can distribute workloads across multiple processing units. This allows for significant speedups compared to sequential processing, especially for computationally intensive tasks or those involving large datasets. Imagine a program analyzing financial data – parallel processing can analyze different segments simultaneously, leading to much faster results.

2. Improved Scalability:

Efficient handling of growing workloads: As user bases and data volumes increase, applications need to adapt. Parallel programming allows us to scale applications horizontally by adding more processing power. This ensures smooth performance even with growing demands, making the application future-proof.

3. Increased Responsiveness:

Smoother user experience: Modern applications often deal with multiple user requests or interact with external resources like databases. Efficient programming techniques, particularly asynchronous programming, can handle these interactions effectively. This prevents the application from becoming unresponsive while waiting for I/O operations, leading to a more pleasant user experience.

4. Better Resource Utilization:

Maximizing processing power: Modern computers typically have multiple cores or processors. Sequential programs often leave these resources untapped. Parallel programming ensures efficient utilization of all available processing units, leading to faster execution and improved overall efficiency.

5. Competitive Edge:

Building high-performance applications: In a competitive software landscape, applications that are fast, responsive, and scalable have a significant advantage. By mastering efficient and parallel programming techniques, developers can create applications that stand out in terms of performance and user experience.

Beyond these core benefits, efficient and parallel programming can also lead to:

Reduced development time: Libraries and frameworks can simplify parallel programming tasks, leading to faster development cycles.

Lower operating costs: By optimizing resource utilization, applications can operate more efficiently, potentially leading to cost savings.

In conclusion, efficient and parallel programming are essential tools for developers in today's demanding computing environment. By unlocking the power of concurrency and parallelism, developers can create high-performance, responsive, and scalable applications that meet the ever-growing needs of users and businesses.

Chapter 2
Core Concepts in Concurrent Programming

Concurrent programming forms the foundation for building efficient and scalable applications. This section dives into the fundamental concepts you'll need to understand to master concurrent programming in Python.

1. Processes vs Threads:

Processes: These are independent units of execution within an operating system. Each process has its own memory space and resources. Processes can communicate with each other through mechanisms like inter-process communication (IPC).

Threads: Threads are lightweight units of execution within a process. They share the same memory space and resources as the main process. This makes threads faster to create and manage compared to processes, but also necessitates careful synchronization to avoid data corruption.

2. The Global Interpreter Lock (GIL):

Python's Global Interpreter Lock (GIL) is an important concept to understand. The GIL ensures that only one thread can execute Python bytecode at a time, even on multi-core systems. This prevents race conditions in applications that heavily rely on manipulating Python objects.

While the GIL limits true parallelism for CPU-bound tasks in Python, it simplifies memory management and debugging for many common programming scenarios.

3. Synchronization Primitives:

Since multiple threads can access shared resources within a process concurrently, synchronization becomes crucial to prevent data corruption and race conditions. Race conditions occur when multiple threads access and modify the same data in an uncontrolled manner, leading to unpredictable results.

Common synchronization primitives in Python include:

Locks (Mutexes): These ensure that only one thread can access a critical section of code at a time.

Semaphores: These control access to a limited number of resources.

Condition variables: These allow threads to wait for specific conditions to be met before proceeding.

4. Communication Mechanisms:

Threads within a process need to communicate to exchange data and coordinate their actions. Here are some common communication mechanisms:

Shared memory: Threads can directly access and modify shared data structures within the process's memory space. However, this requires careful synchronization to avoid data corruption.

Messaging: Threads can send and receive messages through queues or channels. This provides a more structured and reliable way for threads to communicate.

5. Understanding Non-Determinism:

Concurrent programs can sometimes exhibit non-deterministic behavior. This means that the final outcome of the program can vary depending on the timing and scheduling of threads. While this can be challenging to reason about, techniques like proper synchronization can help mitigate non-determinism and ensure predictable program behavior.

By mastering these core concepts, you'll be well-equipped to leverage the power of concurrency and parallelism in your Python applications. The following chapters will delve deeper into specific techniques and libraries for implementing concurrent programming in Python.

2.1 Threads and Processes: Units of Execution

In the realm of concurrent programming, processes and threads are the fundamental building blocks for executing tasks. Understanding the distinction between them is crucial for making informed decisions when designing concurrent applications in Python.

Processes:

Independent Executions: Processes are heavyweight entities that represent independent units of execution within an operating system. Each process has its own dedicated memory space, containing its program code, data, and resources like open files. This isolation ensures that processes don't interfere with each other's memory and avoids conflicts.

Resource Management: The operating system manages processes, allocating them resources like CPU time and memory. Processes can be created, terminated, and suspended by the operating system. This management adds some overhead compared to threads, but it also provides a robust layer of separation and security.

Communication: While processes are independent, they can still communicate with each other using mechanisms like inter-process communication (IPC). This allows processes to exchange data and synchronize their actions. However, IPC can be complex to implement compared to thread communication.

Threads:

Lightweight Units: Threads are lightweight units of execution that exist within a process. Unlike processes, multiple threads share the same memory space and resources of the parent process. This makes them faster to create and manage compared to processes.

Shared Resources: Since threads share memory, they can efficiently access and modify the same data structures. However, this shared access necessitates careful synchronization to prevent race conditions and data corruption. Synchronization primitives like locks and semaphores become essential for thread safety.

Context Switching: The operating system can rapidly switch between different threads within the same process. This rapid switching creates the illusion of concurrency, where multiple threads appear to be running simultaneously even on a single CPU.

Choosing Between Processes and Threads:

The decision of using processes or threads depends on your specific needs:

Isolation and Security: If your application requires strong isolation between different tasks or needs to protect critical resources, processes are the better choice.

Performance for CPU-bound tasks: While the GIL in Python limits true parallelism for CPU-bound tasks using threads, they can still offer some performance benefits when dealing with I/O bound operations.

Memory Usage: Processes require more memory due to their dedicated memory space, while threads share the memory of the parent process.

Development Complexity: Managing thread communication and synchronization can add complexity to your code compared to processes.

In essence:

Processes offer strong isolation and resource management, while threads provide lightweight and efficient execution within a process. By understanding these characteristics, you can choose the right unit of execution for your concurrent programming needs in Python. The following sections will explore how to leverage these concepts for effective parallel and concurrent programming.

2.2 The Global Interpreter Lock (GIL) and its Implications

The Global Interpreter Lock (GIL) is a unique feature of the CPython implementation of Python, the most widely used Python interpreter. It acts as a kind of traffic cop for Python bytecode execution, ensuring that only one thread can execute Python bytecode at a time, even on multi-core processors.

Why the GIL Exists:

The GIL was introduced for a few key reasons:

Simplified Memory Management: Python uses reference counting for memory management. The GIL ensures that only one thread can modify reference counts at a time, preventing race conditions and data corruption that could occur if multiple threads tried to manipulate the same object's reference count simultaneously.

Thread Safety for Built-in Functions: Many built-in Python functions and data structures are not thread-safe. The GIL prevents multiple threads from accessing and modifying these functions or structures concurrently, simplifying development and avoiding potential issues.

Implications of the GIL:

While the GIL offers some benefits, it also has significant implications for parallel programming in Python:

Limited Parallelism for CPU-bound tasks: Since only one thread can execute Python bytecode at a time, the GIL restricts true parallelism for CPU-bound tasks that heavily rely on the CPU for calculations. Even on a multi-core system, only one core can be truly utilized for Python bytecode execution at a time.

Impact on Performance: For tasks that are heavily reliant on CPU power, the GIL can become a bottleneck, limiting the potential speedups achievable through multithreading.

Mitigating the Impact of the GIL:

Despite the limitations, there are ways to work around the GIL and still leverage concurrency in Python applications:

Focus on I/O-bound tasks: The GIL has less impact on I/O-bound tasks, where the program spends most of its time waiting for external resources like network requests or disk I/O. Here, multithreading can still be beneficial by allowing different threads to handle waiting for I/O operations concurrently.

Utilize Multiprocessing: For truly CPU-bound tasks, Python's multiprocessing module allows you to create separate processes, each with its own GIL. This enables true parallelism across multiple cores, as each process can execute Python bytecode independently.

Alternative Implementations: If the GIL is a major obstacle for your project, consider alternative Python implementations like PyPy, which does not have a GIL and can potentially offer better performance for CPU-bound tasks.

Conclusion:

The GIL is a fundamental aspect of the CPython interpreter. Understanding its purpose and limitations is crucial for effectively utilizing concurrency and parallelism in Python. While it restricts true parallelism for CPU-bound tasks, it simplifies development and ensures thread safety for many common use cases. By employing strategies like focusing on I/O-bound tasks, utilizing multiprocessing, or exploring alternative implementations when necessary, you can still leverage the power of concurrency in your Python applications.

.

2.3 Synchronization Primitives: Semaphores, Mutexes, and More

In the world of concurrent programming, where multiple threads or processes access shared resources, chaos can quickly ensue without proper coordination. This is where synchronization primitives come in – essential tools for ensuring data consistency and preventing race conditions.

A race condition occurs when multiple threads access and modify the same data in an uncontrolled manner, leading to unpredictable outcomes. Synchronization primitives act as traffic controllers, dictating access to shared resources and ensuring that only one thread can operate on critical sections of code at a time.

Here are some key synchronization primitives in Python:

Locks (Mutexes):

A mutex (mutual exclusion) is a fundamental synchronization primitive. It acts like a lock on a door. Only one thread can acquire the lock at a time. Any other thread attempting to acquire the lock will be blocked until the first thread releases it.
This ensures that only one thread can access a critical section of code that modifies shared data, preventing race conditions.
The threading.Lock class in Python provides mutex functionality.

Semaphores:

Semaphores are a generalization of mutexes. They control access to a limited number of resources, not just one. Imagine a pool of bicycles; a semaphore can act as a counter that keeps track of how many bikes are available.

A thread can acquire the semaphore if there are available resources (bikes). Otherwise, it will be blocked until a resource becomes free (a bike is returned).

Semaphores are useful for scenarios where multiple threads need to access a limited pool of resources, ensuring fair and controlled access.

The threading.Semaphore class provides semaphore functionality in Python.

Condition Variables:

While locks and semaphores control access to resources, condition variables allow threads to wait for specific conditions to be met before proceeding. Imagine waiting for a signal at a busy intersection.

A thread can wait on a condition variable, and another thread can signal that the condition is now true (the light has turned green).

Condition variables are often used in conjunction with locks to create more complex synchronization patterns.

The threading.Condition class provides condition variable functionality in Python.

Event Objects:

Event objects are simple flags that can be set or cleared. Threads can wait on an event object to become set before proceeding.

This allows one thread to signal another that a certain task has been completed or a specific condition has been met.

Event objects are useful for simple notification scenarios between threads.

The threading.Event class provides event object functionality in Python.

Choosing the Right Primitive:

The choice of synchronization primitive depends on your specific needs:

Mutual exclusion: Use a mutex (lock) to ensure only one thread can access a critical section of code.

Limited resources: Use a semaphore to control access to a pool of limited resources.

Waiting for conditions: Use a condition variable to wait for specific conditions to be met before proceeding.

Simple notifications: Use an event object to signal another thread that a task has been completed.

Beyond these core primitives, Python offers additional synchronization mechanisms like atomic operations and reader-writer locks. Understanding these primitives and their applications is essential for writing thread-safe and concurrent Python programs.

2.4 Communication Mechanisms: Data Sharing and Message Passing

In the realm of concurrent programming, where multiple threads or processes work together, effective communication is paramount. Threads within a process and processes themselves need to exchange data and synchronize their actions. Here, we explore two key communication mechanisms: data sharing and message passing.

1. Data Sharing:

Shared Memory: This approach allows threads within a process to directly access and modify the same data structures in the process's memory space. This can be a very efficient way for threads to communicate, as data can be accessed and updated quickly.

Benefits:

Fast communication: Direct access to shared data enables rapid data exchange between threads.
Efficient for small data: Sharing small data structures can be more efficient than sending messages.

Challenges:

Race conditions: Without proper synchronization, concurrent access to shared data can lead to race conditions and data corruption. Careful use of synchronization primitives like locks and semaphores is crucial.
Complexity: Managing synchronization logic for complex data sharing scenarios can increase code complexity.

2. Message Passing:

Structured Communication: This approach involves sending and receiving messages between threads or processes. Messages can contain data, instructions, or control signals. Threads or processes communicate by placing messages in queues or channels.

Benefits:

Improved reliability: Message passing decouples sender and receiver, reducing the risk of race conditions and data corruption.
Scalability: Message passing is well-suited for distributed systems where processes communicate across a network.
Flexibility: Messages can encapsulate complex data structures and control information.

Challenges:

Overhead: Sending and receiving messages can introduce some overhead compared to direct data access.
Complexity: Implementing message passing protocols and managing message queues can add complexity to the code.

Choosing the Right Mechanism:

The choice between data sharing and message passing depends on several factors:

Complexity of communication: For simple data exchange within a process, shared memory can be efficient. For more complex communication patterns or distributed systems, message passing is preferred.

Need for isolation: If strong isolation between threads or processes is required, message passing offers a more robust communication model.

Performance requirements: For performance-critical scenarios where speed is paramount, data sharing might be preferable (with careful synchronization).

In conclusion, both data sharing and message passing offer valuable tools for communication in concurrent programs. By understanding their strengths and weaknesses, you can choose the right mechanism to achieve efficient and reliable communication in your Python applications. The following chapters will delve deeper into specific libraries and techniques for implementing these communication mechanisms in Python.

Part 2: Mastering Parallel Programming Techniques

Chapter 3
Multithreading in Python

Multithreading is a powerful technique in concurrent programming that allows you to run multiple threads within a single process. This can significantly improve the performance of your application by enabling tasks to be executed concurrently, especially for I/O bound operations.

Here's a breakdown of multithreading in Python:

1. The threading Module:

Python provides the threading module for creating and managing threads. This module offers functionalities like:

Thread Class: This class represents a thread of execution. You can create a thread object by specifying the target function and any arguments it should take.
start() Method: This method starts the execution of the thread.

join() Method: This method waits for a thread to finish execution before continuing with the main program.

Synchronization Primitives: The module also provides synchronization primitives like locks and semaphores to ensure thread safety and prevent race conditions.

2. Creating and Running Threads:

Here's a basic example of creating and running a thread in Python:

```python
Python
import threading

def some_function(arg):
  # Simulate some work being done
  print(f"Doing some work in thread with argument: {arg}")
  for i in range(3):
    print(f"Thread {threading.get_ident()} working: {i}")

# Create a thread object
my_thread   =   threading.Thread(target=some_function,
args=("hello",))

# Start the thread execution
```

```
my_thread.start()

# Wait for the thread to finish (optional)
my_thread.join()

print("Main program finished!")
```
Use code with caution.

content_copy

3. Thread Safety Considerations:

When working with multiple threads, it's crucial to ensure thread safety. This means your program's data and behavior remain consistent even when accessed by multiple threads concurrently. Here's how to achieve thread safety:

Synchronization: Use synchronization primitives like locks and semaphores to control access to shared resources and prevent race conditions.

Immutable Data: When possible, use immutable data structures like tuples and strings as they can't be modified by threads, reducing the risk of data corruption.

4. Common Threading Patterns:

Several common threading patterns can be employed for various scenarios:

The Producer-Consumer Pattern: This pattern involves one thread (producer) creating data and placing it in a buffer, while another thread (consumer) retrieves and processes the data.
The Thread Pool Pattern: This pattern creates a pool of worker threads that can be reused for executing tasks submitted to the pool.

5. When to Use Multithreading:

Multithreading is beneficial for applications that involve:

I/O-bound tasks: Operations like waiting for network requests or disk access can be handled efficiently with multiple threads, as other threads can continue execution while waiting for I/O.

CPU-bound tasks (with limitations): While the GIL (Global Interpreter Lock) in Python limits true parallelism for CPU-bound tasks, multithreading can still provide some performance improvements by allowing threads to handle waiting periods efficiently.

6. Limitations of Multithreading:

Here are some limitations to consider when using multithreading:

Complexity: Managing multiple threads and ensuring thread safety can add complexity to your code.
Overhead: Creating and managing threads introduces some overhead compared to sequential execution.

In conclusion, multithreading is a valuable tool for improving the responsiveness and performance of Python applications. By understanding the concepts, utilizing the threading module effectively, and addressing thread safety concerns, you can leverage the power of concurrency to create efficient and scalable Python programs.

3.1 The threading Module: Creating and Managing Threads

Python's threading module provides the foundation for implementing multithreading in your applications. It offers functionalities for creating, managing, and synchronizing threads to achieve concurrent execution of tasks.

Key Components of the threading Module:

Thread Class: This class represents a unit of execution within a process. You can create a Thread object by specifying the target function it should execute and any arguments it needs.

Python
```
import threading

def some_function(arg):
  # Simulate some work being done
  print(f"Doing some work with argument: {arg}")
  # ... your function logic here

# Create a thread object
my_thread    =    threading.Thread(target=some_function,
args=("hello",))
```
Use code with caution.
content_copy

start() Method: This method initiates the execution of the thread. Once you call start(), the thread becomes a separate flow of control within the process.

Python

```
# Start the thread execution
my_thread.start()
```

Use code with caution.

content_copy

join() Method: This method pauses the execution of the main program until the target thread finishes its work. This ensures that the main program doesn't continue until the thread completes its task.

Python

```
# Wait for the thread to finish (optional)
my_thread.join()

print("Main program finished!")
```

Use code with caution.

content_copy

Managing Thread Execution:

is_alive() Method: This method checks if a thread is still running (hasn't finished execution).

daemon Property: Setting the daemon property to True indicates that the thread is a background service and should not prevent the program from exiting when the main thread finishes.

Thread Termination: While Python doesn't provide a standard way to directly terminate a thread, you can use techniques like setting flags or utilizing events to signal a thread to stop its execution gracefully.

Synchronization Primitives:

The threading module also provides essential tools for ensuring thread safety and preventing race conditions:

Locks (Mutexes): Represented by the threading.Lock class, locks provide exclusive access to critical sections of code, ensuring only one thread can modify shared data at a time.
Semaphores: Implemented by the threading.Semaphore class, semaphores control access to a limited pool of resources, preventing multiple threads from exceeding a certain usage limit.
Condition Variables: The threading.Condition class allows threads to wait for specific conditions to be met before

proceeding. This is useful for implementing more complex synchronization patterns.

Beyond the Basics:

The threading module offers additional functionalities like:

Timer Class: This class allows you to schedule functions to be executed after a certain time delay or at regular intervals.
local Module: This module provides thread-local storage, enabling threads to store data specific to their context without worrying about conflicts with other threads.
Effectively utilizing the threading module and its components is crucial for creating well-structured, concurrent Python programs. Remember, while multithreading can improve performance, it also introduces complexity. Careful planning, thread safety considerations, and proper synchronization are essential for reaping the benefits of multithreading without introducing errors or unexpected behavior.

3.2 Synchronization in Multithreaded Applications

In the realm of multithreaded programming, where multiple threads access shared resources concurrently, synchronization becomes the cornerstone of ensuring data integrity and predictable program behavior. Without proper synchronization, race conditions can arise, leading to corrupted data and unpredictable outcomes.

Understanding Race Conditions:

A race condition occurs when multiple threads access and modify the same data in an uncontrolled manner. The outcome depends on the timing and scheduling of these threads, leading to inconsistencies and potential errors.

Imagine a bank account scenario:

Thread 1 tries to withdraw $100.
Before the withdrawal is complete, Thread 2 checks the balance.
If the program lacks synchronization, the balance might appear to be higher than it actually is, leading to an incorrect withdrawal by Thread 2 and potentially negative account balance.

Synchronization Primitives: Ensuring Order

To prevent such issues, synchronization primitives come into play. These act as tools for coordinating access to shared resources and enforcing a specific order of execution for critical sections of code. Here are some key synchronization primitives in Python's threading module:

Locks (Mutexes):

A mutex (mutual exclusion) ensures that only one thread can acquire a lock at a time. Any other thread attempting to acquire the lock will be blocked until the first thread releases it.

This guarantees exclusive access to a critical section of code, preventing race conditions.
The threading.Lock class provides mutex functionality in Python.

Semaphores:

Semaphores are a generalization of mutexes. They control access to a limited number of resources, not just one.

Imagine a pool of bicycles; a semaphore can act as a counter that keeps track of how many bikes are available.

A thread can acquire the semaphore if there are available resources (bikes). Otherwise, it will be blocked until a resource becomes free (a bike is returned).

The threading.Semaphore class provides semaphore functionality in Python.

Condition Variables:

While locks and semaphores control access to resources, condition variables allow threads to wait for specific conditions to be met before proceeding.

Imagine waiting for a signal at a busy intersection. A thread can wait on a condition variable, and another thread can signal that the condition is now true (the light has turned green).

Condition variables are often used in conjunction with locks to create more complex synchronization patterns.

The threading.Condition class provides condition variable functionality in Python.

Choosing the Right Synchronization Primitive:

The selection of the appropriate synchronization primitive depends on your specific needs:

Mutual exclusion: Use a lock (mutex) to ensure only one thread can access a critical section of code that modifies shared data.

Limited resources: Use a semaphore to control access to a pool of limited resources.

Waiting for conditions: Use a condition variable to wait for specific conditions to be met before proceeding.

Common Synchronization Patterns:

Beyond these primitives, various synchronization patterns can be implemented to manage complex scenarios:

The Producer-Consumer Pattern: This pattern involves one thread (producer) creating data and placing it in a buffer, while another thread (consumer) retrieves and processes the data. Synchronization ensures proper data placement and retrieval from the buffer.

The Reader-Writer Lock: This lock allows concurrent read access for multiple threads but provides exclusive access for writing, preventing conflicts when multiple threads attempt to modify the data simultaneously.

Beyond the threading Module:

While the threading module offers core synchronization primitives, Python also provides libraries like:

concurrent.futures: This module offers higher-level abstractions for managing concurrent tasks, including synchronization mechanisms.

Third-party libraries: Libraries like syncio provide alternative approaches to synchronization and asynchronous programming.

In conclusion, synchronization is an essential concept in multithreaded programming. By understanding race conditions, utilizing synchronization primitives effectively, and employing appropriate patterns, you can develop robust and predictable concurrent applications in Python.

Remember, well-placed synchronization safeguards your program's data integrity and ensures reliable behavior, even in the presence of multiple threads.

3.3 Common Threading Patterns and Best Practices

Multithreading offers a powerful approach to improve application performance and responsiveness in Python. However, it also introduces complexity and potential pitfalls. To leverage its benefits effectively, understanding common threading patterns and best practices is crucial.

Here's a breakdown of some key patterns and practices to consider:

1. The Producer-Consumer Pattern:

Scenario: This pattern is ideal for situations where one thread (producer) generates data and places it in a buffer (like a queue), while another thread (consumer) retrieves and processes the data.
Synchronization: Proper synchronization is essential to ensure the producer doesn't overflow the buffer and the

consumer retrieves valid data. Techniques like locks or semaphores can be used.

Implementation: You can implement the buffer using a queue data structure from the queue module or a custom solution with synchronization.

2. The Thread Pool Pattern:

Scenario: This pattern maintains a pool of worker threads that can be reused to execute tasks submitted to the pool. It's efficient for handling many short-lived tasks.

Benefits: Reduces overhead of creating and destroying threads for each task. Improves resource utilization by reusing existing threads.

Implementation: The concurrent.futures module provides higher-level abstractions for managing thread pools and task execution.

3. The Master-Worker Pattern:

'Scenario: This pattern involves a master thread that distributes tasks among multiple worker threads. Worker threads complete the tasks and report results back to the master.

Benefits: Allows for flexible task distribution and workload balancing.

Implementation: You can use the threading module to create worker threads and mechanisms like queues or callbacks for task communication.

.

4. Best Practices for Threading:

Favor Immutability: When possible, use immutable data structures (like tuples or strings) for shared data. This reduces the risk of race conditions as these data structures cannot be modified by threads.

Minimize Synchronization: Use synchronization only when necessary to protect critical sections. Excessive synchronization can introduce overhead and hinder performance.

Favor Thread Communication: If possible, leverage communication mechanisms like queues or channels for thread interaction instead of relying heavily on shared memory. This can improve code maintainability and reduce complexity.

Consider Alternatives: In some cases, asynchronous programming with libraries like asyncio might be a better choice than multithreading, especially for I/O-bound tasks.

5. Debugging and Error Handling:

Debugging multithreaded applications can be challenging due to the non-deterministic nature of thread scheduling. Utilize logging and print statements strategically to track thread behavior.

Consider using debuggers with support for multithreading to step through code execution and identify issues.
Implement robust error handling mechanisms to gracefully manage exceptions that might arise within threads.

By understanding these patterns, best practices, and potential challenges, you can effectively leverage multithreading to create performant and well-structured concurrent applications in Python. Remember, responsible use of threads and careful planning are essential for reaping the benefits of concurrency without introducing errors or unexpected behavior.

3.4 Case Study: Utilizing Multithreading for Web Scraping

Web scraping involves extracting data from websites. It can be a valuable technique for gathering information for various purposes. However, making numerous requests to a website in rapid succession can overload the server and violate terms of service. Here's how multithreading can be effectively used for web scraping while adhering to responsible practices:

Challenges of Sequential Scraping:

Server Overload: Sending too many requests from a single source (IP address) in a short period can overload the website's server.
Slow Performance: Scraping large websites serially can be time-consuming, especially if there are many pages to extract data from.

Benefits of Multithreading:

Parallel Requests: By using multiple threads, you can distribute website requests across threads, reducing the load on the server from a single source.
Improved Performance: Scraping can be significantly faster as multiple threads can fetch data concurrently.

Responsible Web Scraping:

Respect Robots.txt: Always adhere to the website's robots.txt exclusion protocol, which specifies URLs or directories that bots should not scrape.

Implement Delays: Introduce delays between requests sent from each thread to avoid overwhelming the server. You can use techniques like sleep timers or waiting mechanisms based on server response times.

Scrape Ethically: Avoid scraping excessive amounts of data or scraping in a way that disrupts the website's functionality.

Example Implementation:

```Python
import threading
import requests
from queue import Queue

def scrape_url(url, queue):
    # Simulate scraping logic
    response = requests.get(url)
```

```python
    # Extract and process data from the response
    data = ...  # Extracted data
    queue.put(data)  # Add extracted data to the queue

def main():
    # Define a list of URLs to scrape
        urls      =       ["https://www.example.com/page1",
"https://www.example.com/page2", ...]

    # Create a queue to store scraped data
    data_queue = Queue()

    # Create threads and assign scraping tasks
    threads = []
    for url in urls:
        thread = threading.Thread(target=scrape_url, args=(url,
data_queue))
        thread.start()
        threads.append(thread)

    # Wait for all threads to finish
    for thread in threads:
        thread.join()

    # Process scraped data from the queue
```

```
while not data_queue.empty():
  data = data_queue.get()
  # Process the extracted data

if __name__ == "__main__":
  main()
```
Use code with caution.

content_copy

In this example:

The scrape_url function simulates scraping logic and adds extracted data to a queue.

The main function creates threads, assigns scraping tasks to each thread, and manages the queue.

Delays can be implemented within the scrape_url function to control the request rate.

Remember: This is a simplified example. Real-world web scraping might involve more sophisticated techniques for handling dynamic content, parsing HTML, and handling potential errors.

Conclusion:

Multithreading can be a valuable tool for web scraping, but it's crucial to use it responsibly and ethically. By adhering to best practices, implementing delays, and respecting robots.txt guidelines, you can leverage the power of multithreading to efficiently scrape data while being a good web citizen.

Chapter 4
Multiprocessing for CPU-Bound Tasks

While multithreading offers a way to improve concurrency in Python, it has limitations for CPU-bound tasks due to the Global Interpreter Lock (GIL). The GIL ensures thread safety for Python bytecode execution, but it also restricts true parallelism on multi-core systems. Here's where multiprocessing comes in, offering a powerful approach for handling CPU-bound tasks effectively.

Understanding the GIL:

The GIL acts as a kind of traffic cop for Python bytecode execution. Only one thread can acquire the GIL and execute Python bytecode at a time, even on a system with multiple cores.

This ensures thread safety for built-in functions and data structures that are not thread-safe, but it limits the potential performance gains from multithreading for CPU-bound tasks.

Multiprocessing: Unleashing Parallelism

The multiprocessing module in Python allows you to create separate processes, each with its own memory space and GIL. This enables true parallel processing across multiple cores.

Each process can execute Python bytecode independently, utilizing different cores on your CPU simultaneously.

Benefits of Multiprocessing:

Improved Performance: For CPU-bound tasks that heavily rely on the CPU for calculations, multiprocessing can significantly improve performance by utilizing multiple cores effectively.

Isolation: Processes offer stronger isolation compared to threads. This can be beneficial for tasks that require access to specific system resources or need to be strictly separated from other processes.

Drawbacks of Multiprocessing:

Overhead: Creating and managing separate processes introduces more overhead compared to threads.

Communication Complexity: Communication and data exchange between processes require careful planning and use of techniques like queues or pipes.

When to Use Multiprocessing:

CPU-bound tasks: If your application involves intensive calculations or computations that heavily utilize the CPU, multiprocessing is the way to go.

Tasks requiring isolation: If your tasks need strong isolation from each other or require access to specific system resources that might not be shared well between threads, processes offer a better approach.

Example: Parallelizing Calculations

```python
Python
import multiprocessing

def calculate(num):
  # Simulate some CPU-bound calculation
  result = 0
  for i in range(1000000):
    result += num * i
```

```python
    return result

def main():
    # Define numbers for calculation
    numbers = [10, 20, 30, 40]

    # Create a pool of worker processes
    pool = multiprocessing.Pool()

    # Distribute calculation tasks to worker processes
    results = pool.map(calculate, numbers)

    # Process the results
    for result in results:
        print(result)

if __name__ == "__main__":
    main()
```

Use code with caution.

content_copy

In this example:

The calculate function performs a CPU-bound calculation.

The main function creates a pool of worker processes using multiprocessing.Pool.

The pool.map function distributes the calculation tasks for each number to the worker processes.

Each process calculates its assigned number independently, utilizing different cores.

Remember: Multiprocessing introduces more complexity compared to multithreading. Evaluate your application's needs and the nature of your tasks to determine if the benefits of true parallelism outweigh the overhead of process creation and management.

Beyond the Basics:

The multiprocessing module offers functionalities like:

Process Class: This class allows you to create and manage individual processes.

.

Queues and Pipes: These mechanisms enable communication and data exchange between processes.

Manager: This class provides tools for creating shared memory objects that can be accessed by multiple processes.

By effectively utilizing multiprocessing, you can harness the power of multiple cores to significantly improve the performance of CPU-bound tasks in your Python applications.

4.1 The multiprocessing Module: Running Processes in Parallel

.

Python's multiprocessing module empowers you to create and manage processes, taking advantage of multiple cores on your system to achieve true parallelism for CPU-bound tasks. This stands in contrast to multithreading, where the Global Interpreter Lock (GIL) restricts true parallelism for Python bytecode execution.

Key Concepts:

Processes vs. Threads: Processes are fundamental units of execution in an operating system, each with its own memory space and resources. Threads, on the other hand, are lightweight units of execution within a single process, sharing the same memory space.

The GIL (Global Interpreter Lock): The GIL ensures thread safety in Python by allowing only one thread to execute Python bytecode at a time. This limits the ability of multithreading to leverage multiple cores effectively for CPU-bound tasks.

Benefits of Multiprocessing:

Parallel Processing: By creating separate processes, each process can run independently on a different CPU core, achieving true parallelism for CPU-bound tasks.

Isolation: Processes offer stronger isolation compared to threads. This can be beneficial for tasks that require access to specific system resources or need to be strictly separated from other processes.

.

Drawbacks of Multiprocessing:

Overhead: Creating and managing separate processes introduces more overhead compared to threads due to the need to allocate memory and resources for each process.

Communication Complexity: Sharing data and communicating between processes requires careful planning and techniques like queues, pipes, or shared memory.

The multiprocessing Module in Action:

The multiprocessing module provides functionalities for creating, managing, and communicating with processes:

Process Class: This class represents a process. You can create a Process object, specifying the target function it should execute and any arguments it needs.

```python
import multiprocessing

def some_function(num):
  # Simulate some CPU-bound work
  result = 0
  for i in range(1000000):
    result += num * i
  return result

def main():
  # Create a process object
  process = multiprocessing.Process(target=some_function, args=(10,))

  # Start the process execution
  process.start()
```

```python
  # Wait for the process to finish (optional)
  process.join()

if __name__ == "__main__":
  main()
```
Use code with caution.
content_copy

Pool Class: The Pool class simplifies managing a pool of worker processes. You can submit tasks to the pool, and it will distribute them among the worker processes efficiently.

Python
```python
import multiprocessing

def calculate(num):
  # Simulate some calculation
  return num * num

def main():
  # Define numbers for calculation
  numbers = [1, 2, 3, 4]

  # Create a pool of worker processes
  pool = multiprocessing.Pool()
```

```
# Distribute calculation tasks to worker processes
results = pool.map(calculate, numbers)

# Process the results
for result in results:
  print(result)

if __name__ == "__main__":
 main()
```
Use code with caution.

content_copy

Inter-Process Communication (IPC):

Queues: Processes can send and receive data messages using queues.

Pipes: Processes can establish unidirectional communication channels using pipes.

Manager: This class provides tools for creating shared memory objects that can be accessed by multiple processes.

Choosing Between Multithreading and Multiprocessing:

CPU-bound tasks: Use multiprocessing for CPU-bound tasks to leverage multiple cores and achieve true parallelism.

I/O-bound tasks: Multithreading can still be beneficial for I/O-bound tasks as the GIL doesn't affect waiting for I/O operations.

Simplicity vs. Complexity: Multithreading offers a simpler approach, while multiprocessing introduces more complexity due to process creation and communication overhead.

In conclusion, the multiprocessing module empowers you to harness the power of multiple cores for CPU-bound tasks in Python applications. By understanding its functionalities, its trade-offs compared to multithreading, and best practices for communication and synchronization, you can effectively utilize multiprocessing to achieve significant performance improvements.

4.2 Inter-Process Communication (IPC) Techniques

In the bustling world of concurrent programming, where multiple programs or threads execute simultaneously, ensuring smooth communication and data exchange becomes paramount. This is where Inter-Process Communication (IPC) comes into play. It acts as a bridge, allowing processes to exchange information and collaborate effectively. Here's a breakdown of some key IPC techniques:

Pipes:

One-way Streams: Pipes establish a one-way communication channel between two related processes. Data flows from a writing process (producer) to a reading process (consumer) in a unidirectional stream.

Anonymous vs. Named Pipes: Anonymous pipes are temporary and only usable by the creating processes. Named pipes, on the other hand, have a specific name, allowing unrelated processes to connect and communicate.

Message Queues:

Flexible Messaging: Message queues provide a more versatile approach to IPC. Processes can send and receive messages asynchronously, meaning the sender doesn't need to wait for the receiver to be ready. Messages are placed in a queue, and receiving processes retrieve them when available.

Benefits: Message queues offer advantages like decoupling sender and receiver, enabling one-to-many or many-to-one communication patterns, and providing message buffering for handling spikes in message traffic.

Shared Memory:

Direct Data Sharing: Shared memory allows processes to directly access and modify the same memory segment. This approach offers high performance for frequently accessed data but requires careful synchronization to avoid data corruption.

Synchronization Primitives: Semaphores, mutexes, and other synchronization primitives are crucial for coordinating access to shared memory and preventing race conditions.

.

Sockets:

Network Communication: Sockets enable communication between processes on the same machine or across a network. They provide a more complex but flexible mechanism for distributed applications.

Connection-Oriented vs. Connectionless: Sockets can be either connection-oriented (TCP) for reliable, stream-based communication or connectionless (UDP) for simpler, datagram-based communication.

Remote Procedure Calls (RPC):

Abstraction over IPC: RPC offers a higher-level abstraction on top of IPC mechanisms. It allows processes to invoke procedures on remote machines as if they were local procedures. This simplifies distributed programming by hiding the underlying communication details.

Choosing the Right Technique:

The optimal IPC technique depends on your specific needs:

For simple data exchange between related processes, pipes might suffice.
Message queues are ideal for asynchronous communication and buffering.
Shared memory offers high performance for frequently accessed data, but use it with caution due to synchronization complexities.
Sockets provide flexibility for network communication.
RPC simplifies distributed programming by abstracting the communication layer.

Additional Considerations:

Security: When choosing an IPC technique, consider security implications. Sockets and RPC might require additional security measures for communication across networks.

Performance: The performance characteristics of each technique vary. Shared memory can be fast, but message queues and RPC might introduce some overhead.
Complexity: The complexity of implementation and usage also differs. Pipes and message queues offer a simpler approach compared to shared memory or RPC.

By understanding these IPC techniques, their strengths and weaknesses, and the factors to consider when choosing one, you can establish effective communication channels between processes, enabling them to work together seamlessly in concurrent systems.

4.3 Memory Management and Data Sharing in Multiprocessing

While multiprocessing offers significant advantages for CPU-bound tasks by leveraging multiple cores, memory management and data sharing present unique challenges compared to multithreading. Here's a breakdown of these considerations:

Memory Management:

Separate Memory Spaces: Processes have their own isolated memory spaces. This ensures strong isolation and prevents accidental data corruption that could occur if multiple threads accessed the same memory location in multithreading.

Copying vs. Sharing: When data needs to be shared between processes, a copy of the data is typically created and passed to the other process. This avoids issues with concurrent modification of the same data in different memory spaces.

Data Sharing Techniques:

Queues and Pipes: These mechanisms enable processes to send and receive messages containing data. Queues are first-in-first-out (FIFO) buffers, while pipes offer unidirectional communication channels.

```python
Python
import multiprocessing
from queue import Queue

def process1(queue):
  # Simulate some work
  data = "Hello from process 1"
  queue.put(data)

def process2(queue):
  # Receive data from queue
  received_data = queue.get()
  print(f"Received data: {received_data}")

def main():
  # Create a queue for communication
  queue = Queue()

  # Create and start processes
```

```python
    p1      =      multiprocessing.Process(target=process1,
args=(queue,))
    p2      =      multiprocessing.Process(target=process2,
args=(queue,))

 p1.start()
 p2.start()

 # Wait for processes to finish
 p1.join()
 p2.join()

if __name__ == "__main__":
 main()
```
Use code with caution.

content_copy

Shared Memory: The multiprocessing module provides
functionalities for creating shared memory segments that
can be accessed by multiple processes. This can be more
efficient for large data structures compared to copying data
through queues or pipes. However, careful synchronization
is crucial to avoid data races and ensure safe access to shared
memory.

Synchronization in Multiprocessing:

Even though processes have separate memory spaces, synchronization is still essential when multiple processes access shared resources like files or external devices. Techniques like semaphores and locks from the multiprocessing module can be used to coordinate access and prevent race conditions.

Key Considerations:

Data Size: When choosing a data sharing method, consider the size of the data. Queues and pipes might be suitable for small data pieces, while shared memory can be more efficient for larger data structures.

Performance: Copying data through queues or pipes can introduce some overhead. Shared memory can offer better performance, but it requires careful synchronization.
Complexity: Implementing shared memory with proper synchronization can add complexity to your code.

In conclusion, memory management and data sharing in multiprocessing require careful planning and consideration. By understanding the concepts of separate memory spaces, data copying vs. sharing techniques, and synchronization mechanisms, you can effectively design and implement multiprocessing applications that leverage multiple cores while maintaining data integrity and avoiding race conditions.

4.4 Case Study: Parallel Image Processing with Multiprocessing

While multiprocessing offers significant advantages for CPU-bound tasks by leveraging multiple cores, memory management and data sharing present unique challenges compared to multithreading. Here's a breakdown of these considerations:

Memory Management:

Separate Memory Spaces: Processes have their own isolated memory spaces. This ensures strong isolation and prevents accidental data corruption that could occur if multiple threads accessed the same memory location in multithreading.

Copying vs. Sharing: When data needs to be shared between processes, a copy of the data is typically created and passed to the other process. This avoids issues with concurrent modification of the same data in different memory spaces.

Data Sharing Techniques:

Queues and Pipes: These mechanisms enable processes to send and receive messages containing data. Queues are first-in-first-out (FIFO) buffers, while pipes offer unidirectional communication channels.

```python
Python
import multiprocessing
from queue import Queue

def process1(queue):
  # Simulate some work
  data = "Hello from process 1"
  queue.put(data)

def process2(queue):
  # Receive data from queue
  received_data = queue.get()
  print(f"Received data: {received_data}")
```

```python
def main():
    # Create a queue for communication
    queue = Queue()

    # Create and start processes
    p1 = multiprocessing.Process(target=process1,
args=(queue,))
    p2 = multiprocessing.Process(target=process2,
args=(queue,))

    p1.start()
    p2.start()

    # Wait for processes to finish
    p1.join()
    p2.join()

if __name__ == "__main__":
    main()
```
Use code with caution.

content_copy

Shared Memory: The multiprocessing module provides functionalities for creating shared memory segments that can be accessed by multiple processes. This can be more efficient for large data structures compared to copying data through queues or pipes. However, careful synchronization is crucial to avoid data races and ensure safe access to shared memory.

Synchronization in Multiprocessing:

Even though processes have separate memory spaces, synchronization is still essential when multiple processes access shared resources like files or external devices. Techniques like semaphores and locks from the multiprocessing module can be used to coordinate access and prevent race conditions.

Key Considerations:

Data Size: When choosing a data sharing method, consider the size of the data. Queues and pipes might be suitable for small data pieces, while shared memory can be more efficient for larger data structures.

Performance: Copying data through queues or pipes can introduce some overhead. Shared memory can offer better performance, but it requires careful synchronization.

Complexity: Implementing shared memory with proper synchronization can add complexity to your code.

In conclusion, memory management and data sharing in multiprocessing require careful planning and consideration. By understanding the concepts of separate memory spaces, data copying vs. sharing techniques, and synchronization mechanisms, you can effectively design and implement multiprocessing applications that leverage multiple cores while maintaining data integrity and avoiding race conditions.

Chapter 5
Asynchronous Programming with asyncio

In the world of web development, responsiveness is king. Users expect applications to feel fast and fluid, even when dealing with multiple requests or waiting for data from external sources. Traditional synchronous programming can struggle in these scenarios, blocking the main thread and potentially hindering user experience. Here's where asynchronous programming with asyncio comes in, offering a powerful approach to building responsive and efficient Python applications.

Understanding Asynchronous Programming:

Synchronous vs. Asynchronous:
Synchronous programming executes tasks one after another. The program waits for one task to finish before moving on to the next.

Asynchronous programming allows your program to initiate multiple tasks concurrently. It doesn't wait for each task to finish completely before starting the next.
Benefits of Asynchronous Programming:

Improved Responsiveness: By not blocking the main thread, your application can remain responsive even while waiting for I/O-bound operations (like network requests or disk access) to complete. The UI stays interactive, and users don't experience delays.

Efficient Resource Utilization: Asynchronous programming allows your program to make better use of system resources. While waiting for tasks to complete, the main thread can handle other tasks or events.

Core Concepts in asyncio:

Coroutines: These are Python functions that can be suspended and resumed later. They are the building blocks of asynchronous programming in asyncio.

Event Loop: The event loop is the heart of asyncio. It manages the execution of coroutines and I/O operations. It schedules coroutines to run when they are ready (e.g., when data arrives from a network request).

Common asyncio Functions:

async def: This keyword declares an asynchronous function, which can be a coroutine.

await: This keyword is used within an async function to suspend its execution until a task (like an I/O operation) completes. The event loop then schedules the coroutine to resume when the awaited task is finished.

Example: Using asyncio for Network Requests:

Python
```python
import asyncio

async def fetch_data(url):
  async with aiohttp.ClientSession() as session:
    async with session.get(url) as response:
     data = await response.text()
     return data

async def main():
    tasks = [fetch_data("https://www.example.com/data1"),
fetch_data("https://www.example.com/data2")]
   results = await asyncio.gather(*tasks)  # Gather results from
all tasks concurrently
  for result in results:
   print(result)
```

```python
if __name__ == "__main__":
    asyncio.run(main())
```
Use code with caution.

content_copy

In this example:

fetch_data is an asynchronous function that fetches data from a URL using the aiohttp library.

await response.text() suspends the coroutine until the network request completes and the response is received.

asyncio.gather allows us to run both network requests concurrently and then gather the results.

Error Handling in asyncio:

Asynchronous code can introduce new challenges for error handling. Techniques like try-except blocks can be used within coroutines to handle exceptions gracefully.

Beyond the Basics:

asyncio.Task: This class represents an asynchronous task that can be managed and monitored.

asyncio.ensure_future: This function can be used to schedule coroutines for execution without necessarily waiting for them to complete.

When to Use asyncio:

Asyncio is ideal for applications that heavily rely on I/O-bound operations, where the program spends a significant amount of time waiting for external events. It's a valuable tool for building responsive web applications, network programming, and working with APIs.

In conclusion, asyncio empowers you to create performant and responsive Python applications by enabling asynchronous programming. By understanding its core concepts, functions, and best practices, you can leverage the power of asyncio to build applications that excel in handling I/O-bound tasks and keeping the user experience smooth.

Sources
info
bootcamp.uxdesign.cc/from-basic-tests-to-advanced-techniq
ues-a-deep-dive-into-python-testing-4e267a2e91e8?source=
rss-------1
github.com/TrustInMe/users_edit_app

5.1 Introduction to Asynchronous Programming

In the fast-paced world of web development, applications need to be lightning-fast and responsive. Users expect web pages to load instantly and interactions to feel smooth, even when dealing with multiple requests or waiting for data from external sources. Traditional synchronous programming, where tasks execute one after another, can struggle in these scenarios. Here's where asynchronous programming comes in, offering a powerful approach to building responsive and efficient applications.

Synchronous vs. Asynchronous Programming:

Synchronous Programming: Imagine a single waiter in a restaurant. The waiter can only take one order at a time. They have to wait for the customer to finish placing their order before they can take the next one. This is synchronous programming - the program waits for one task to finish before moving on to the next.

Asynchronous Programming: Now imagine a restaurant with multiple waiters. They can take orders from multiple customers simultaneously, improving efficiency. Asynchronous programming works similarly. It allows your program to initiate multiple tasks concurrently without waiting for each one to finish completely before starting the next.

Benefits of Asynchronous Programming:

Improved Responsiveness: By not blocking the main thread (the waiter taking orders), your application can remain responsive even while waiting for external events (like data from a server) to complete. The UI stays interactive, and users don't experience delays.
Efficient Resource Utilization: Asynchronous programming allows your program to make better use of system resources. While waiting for tasks to complete (like waiting for data to download), the main thread can handle other tasks or events (like processing user input).

Key Concepts in Asynchronous Programming:

Coroutines: These are special Python functions that can be paused and resumed later. They are the building blocks of asynchronous programming. Think of them as waiters who can take multiple orders and come back to them later when the food is ready.

Event Loop: This is the central coordinator in asynchronous programming. It's like the restaurant manager who keeps track of all the waiters' activities and schedules them to take orders, deliver food, etc. The event loop manages the execution of coroutines and I/O operations (like network requests), scheduling them to run when they are ready (e.g., when data arrives from a network request).

Getting Started with Asynchronous Programming:

The specific approach to asynchronous programming will vary depending on the programming language you're using. However, the core concepts remain similar. In Python, the asyncio library provides a powerful framework for building asynchronous applications.

Beyond the Basics:

Asynchronous programming offers a range of techniques and functionalities beyond the fundamentals. Here are some additional concepts to explore:

Error Handling: Asynchronous code introduces new challenges for error handling. Techniques like try-except blocks can be used within coroutines to handle exceptions gracefully.

Advanced asyncio features: asyncio offers functionalities like asyncio.Task (for managing asynchronous tasks) and asyncio.ensure_future (for scheduling coroutines without waiting for them to complete).

When to Use Asynchronous Programming:

Asyncio is particularly beneficial for applications that heavily rely on I/O-bound operations, where the program spends a significant amount of time waiting for external events (like network requests, database interactions, or user input). It's a valuable tool for building responsive web applications, network programming, and working with APIs.

In conclusion, asynchronous programming empowers you to create performant and responsive applications by enabling your program to handle multiple tasks concurrently. By understanding the core concepts and benefits of asynchronous programming, you can unlock its potential to build applications that excel in user experience.

5.2 Event Loops and Coroutines in asyncio

In the realm of asynchronous programming with Python's asyncio library, two fundamental concepts orchestrate the magic: event loops and coroutines. Let's delve into their roles and how they work together to build responsive and efficient applications.

Event Loops: The Maestro of Asynchronous Tasks

Imagine an orchestra conductor. The conductor doesn't play any instruments themselves, but they coordinate the entire ensemble, ensuring each musician plays their part at the right time. The asyncio event loop plays a similar role.

Core Responsibilities:

Schedules coroutines for execution.
Manages I/O operations (like network requests, file I/O).

Monitors for events that signal coroutines can resume (e.g., data arrives from a network request).

Ensures only one coroutine executes at a time on the main thread (due to the Global Interpreter Lock in Python).

Non-Blocking Operations: The event loop doesn't wait for I/O operations to complete before moving on. It can schedule other tasks while waiting for an operation to finish. This is crucial for maintaining responsiveness.

Coroutines: The Asynchronous Actors

Think of coroutines as the individual musicians in the orchestra. Each coroutine represents a unit of work within your asynchronous program.

Characteristics:

Defined using the async def keyword.

Can be suspended and resumed later using the await keyword.

Don't block the event loop when waiting for I/O operations. Instead, they yield control back to the event loop, allowing it to schedule other tasks.

The await Keyword: This keyword is the essence of asynchronous programming. When a coroutine encounters an I/O operation (like await asyncio.sleep(1) or waiting for a network request), it yields control back to the event loop.

The event loop then schedules another coroutine or task while waiting for the I/O operation to complete. Once the operation is finished, the event loop resumes the coroutine at the await point.

The Asynchronous Symphony:

The event loop and coroutines work in perfect harmony:

Coroutine Starts: An asynchronous function (defined with async def) is called, creating a coroutine object.

Event Loop Takes Charge: The event loop schedules the coroutine for execution.

Coroutine Execution: The coroutine runs until it encounters an await expression.

Yielding Control: When await is encountered, the coroutine yields control back to the event loop.

Event Loop in Action: The event loop schedules another coroutine or task while waiting for the I/O operation associated with the await expression to finish.

Resuming the Coroutine: Once the I/O operation completes, the event loop resumes the coroutine's execution from the point where it yielded control.

Coroutine Completion: The coroutine continues execution until it finishes.

In essence, the event loop ensures efficient task management, while coroutines perform the actual work, seamlessly handling I/O operations without blocking the program.

Beyond the Basics:

asyncio.Task: This class represents an asynchronous task that can be managed and monitored within the event loop.

Error Handling: While the event loop manages execution flow, proper error handling within coroutines using try-except blocks is crucial for robust asynchronous applications.

By understanding event loops and coroutines, you can leverage the power of asyncio to build performant and responsive Python applications that excel in handling I/O-bound tasks and keeping the user experience smooth.

5.3 Handling I/O Bound Operations Efficiently

In the world of programming, efficiency is king, especially when dealing with I/O (Input/Output) bound operations. These operations involve waiting for external resources like network requests, disk access, or user input, and can significantly slow down your application if not handled effectively. Here are some key strategies to tackle I/O bound operations efficiently:

Understanding I/O Bound Operations:

CPU vs. I/O Bound: CPU-bound operations involve intensive calculations that utilize the processor heavily. I/O bound operations, on the other hand, spend most of their time waiting for external resources, making the CPU idle.

The Bottleneck: I/O bound operations can become bottlenecks in your application, hindering overall performance.

Strategies for Efficient Handling:

Asynchronous Programming: This approach allows your program to initiate multiple tasks concurrently, even if some are waiting for I/O. The program doesn't block the main thread, keeping the UI responsive. Libraries like asyncio in Python empower asynchronous programming.

Non-Blocking I/O: Techniques like select, poll, or epoll (depending on the language) allow your program to check for multiple I/O events simultaneously without blocking. This enables it to handle other tasks while waiting for I/O to complete.

Minimize I/O Operations: Analyze your code to identify unnecessary I/O calls. Can you combine multiple requests into one? Can you cache frequently accessed data to reduce disk reads?

Batching Operations: Group multiple small I/O operations into a single larger operation. This can improve efficiency, especially for disk access or network requests.

Leverage Multiprocessing: For CPU-bound tasks that occur alongside I/O bound operations, consider using multiprocessing to utilize multiple cores on your system for parallel processing. This can improve overall performance.

Optimizing I/O Operations:

Hardware Upgrades: In some cases, investing in faster storage devices or network connections can provide a significant performance boost for I/O bound operations.

Database Optimization: Ensure your database is properly indexed and queries are efficient. This can significantly reduce I/O wait times when fetching data.

Choosing the Right Approach:

The best approach for handling I/O bound operations depends on your specific application and programming language. Here's a general guideline:

For simple I/O: Non-blocking I/O techniques or minimizing I/O operations might suffice.

For complex I/O scenarios or highly responsive applications: Asynchronous programming with frameworks like asyncio can be highly beneficial.

For CPU-bound tasks alongside I/O: Consider a combination of asynchronous programming and multiprocessing.

Remember: Efficiently handling I/O bound operations is crucial for building performant and responsive applications. By understanding the problem, applying the right strategies, and optimizing your code, you can ensure your application keeps up with user demands and delivers a smooth user experience.

5.4 Building Responsive and Scalable Network Applications

In today's digital landscape, network applications are the backbone of many online interactions. From web services to chat applications, responsiveness and scalability are fundamental qualities for a successful application. Here's a breakdown of key strategies to achieve these goals:

Responsiveness: Keeping Users Engaged

Fast Response Times: Users expect applications to feel snappy and responsive. Aim for low latency by optimizing code and minimizing server-side processing times.

Asynchronous Programming: Techniques like asyncio in Python allow your application to handle multiple requests concurrently without blocking the main thread. This keeps the UI responsive even while waiting for data from external sources.

Client-Side Caching: Store frequently accessed data on the user's device to reduce the need for repeated network requests and improve perceived responsiveness.

Scalability: Handling Growing Demands

Microservices Architecture: Break down your application into smaller, independent services that communicate through APIs. This allows for horizontal scaling of individual services based on their specific needs.

Cloud-Based Infrastructure: Leverage cloud platforms that offer on-demand resource allocation. You can easily scale up or down resources (CPU, memory, storage) as your application's traffic fluctuates.

Load Balancing: Distribute incoming traffic across multiple servers to prevent overloading any single server and ensure smooth performance under heavy loads.

Beyond the Basics

Database Optimization: Ensure your database is properly indexed and queries are efficient. This can significantly reduce I/O wait times and improve overall responsiveness.

Content Delivery Networks (CDNs): Deliver static content (images, JavaScript, CSS) from geographically distributed servers closer to users. This reduces latency and improves user experience.

Monitoring and Alerting: Continuously monitor your application's performance and resource utilization. Set up alerts to notify you of any potential issues that could impact scalability or responsiveness.

Security: Scalability and responsiveness shouldn't come at the expense of security. Implement robust security measures throughout your network application architecture.

Choosing the Right Approach

The optimal approach depends on the type and complexity of your network application:

For simpler applications: Start with a well-optimized architecture on a single server. You can scale up resources as needed.

For large-scale applications with high traffic: Microservices architecture and cloud-based infrastructure become more beneficial for managing complexity and enabling horizontal scaling.

Remember: Building responsive and scalable network applications is an ongoing process. As your application grows and evolves, you'll need to continuously evaluate and adapt your architecture to meet the changing demands.

Additional Considerations

API Design: Design well-documented and efficient APIs for communication between services in a microservices architecture.

Caching Strategies: Implement effective caching mechanisms at different layers (client-side, server-side) to reduce database load and improve performance.

Performance Testing: Regularly test your application under load to identify bottlenecks and areas for improvement.

By adopting these strategies and considerations, you can create well-structured, responsive, and scalable network applications that can handle increasing user demands while delivering a seamless user experience.

5.5 Case Study: Asynchronous Web Server with asyncio

In this case study, we'll explore how asyncio can be leveraged to build a responsive and efficient web server in Python. Traditional web servers using blocking I/O can struggle to handle a high volume of concurrent requests, leading to performance issues and a poor user experience. Asyncio offers a powerful alternative by enabling asynchronous handling of incoming requests.

Scenario:

Imagine a simple web server that serves static content (HTML files) and performs a lightweight database lookup for each request. The goal is to build a responsive server that can handle numerous concurrent requests efficiently.

Implementation with asyncio:

Dependencies: We'll use the asyncio library for asynchronous programming and the aiohttp library for building the web server.

```python
Python
import asyncio
from aiohttp import web
Use code with caution.
content_copy
```

Database Lookup Function (asynchronous):

```python
Python
async def fetch_data(user_id):
    # Simulate a database lookup (replace with your actual logic)
    await asyncio.sleep(0.1)  # Simulate some processing time
    return f"Data for user {user_id}"
Use code with caution.
```

content_copy

Handler Function (asynchronous):
Python
```python
async def handle_request(request):
  user_id = request.match_info.get('user_id')
  data = await fetch_data(user_id)
  response = web.Response(text=data)
  return response
```
Use code with caution.
content_copy

This function handles incoming requests.

It extracts the user_id from the request path.

It calls the fetch_data function asynchronously to retrieve user data.

It constructs and returns an HTTP response with the retrieved data.

Creating the Asynchronous Application:
Python
```python
async def main():
  app = web.Application()
  app.add_routes([web.get('/users/{user_id}', handle_request)])
```

```python
    runner = web.AppRunner(app)
    await runner.setup()
        await runner.aiter(web.Server(runner, host='localhost',
port=8080))
    print("Server started on http://localhost:8080")
    await runner.cleanup()

if __name__ == "__main__":
    asyncio.run(main())
```
Use code with caution.

content_copy

This code creates an aiohttp application object (app).
It defines a route that maps the /users/{user_id} path to the
handle_request function.
It creates an AppRunner object to manage the server.
The await keyword is used throughout to ensure
asynchronous execution.

Benefits of using asyncio:

Improved Responsiveness: By handling requests
asynchronously, the server can process multiple requests
concurrently without blocking. This keeps the server
responsive even under high load.

Efficient Resource Utilization: While waiting for I/O operations (like database lookups), the server can handle other requests, maximizing resource utilization.

Additional Considerations:

Error Handling: Implement proper error handling mechanisms within your asynchronous functions using try-except blocks.

Security: Always prioritize security measures in your web application, even in an asynchronous context.

Scalability: For larger applications, consider incorporating techniques like connection pooling for database interactions or using a framework like aiohttp-redis for caching frequently accessed data.

Conclusion:

This case study demonstrates how asyncio can be a valuable tool for building responsive and efficient web servers in Python. By embracing asynchronous programming, you can create applications that can handle high volumes of concurrent requests while delivering a smooth user experience. Remember to adapt and extend this approach based on your specific web application requirements.

Part 3: Performance Optimization and Scalable Design

Chapter 6
Profiling and Performance Analysis

In the realm of software development, performance is paramount. Even the most elegant code can grind to a halt if it's not optimized. Profiling and performance analysis are essential techniques for identifying bottlenecks and optimizing your Python applications for speed and efficiency.

What is Profiling?

Profiling involves measuring how your program executes. It gathers data on various aspects, such as:

Function calls: How often each function is called and how long it takes to execute.
Line-by-line execution: Time spent executing each line of code.

Memory allocation: How much memory is allocated by different parts of your program.

Why is Profiling Important?

Identify Bottlenecks: Profiling helps pinpoint the sections of your code that take the most time or memory, allowing you to focus optimization efforts on the areas that will yield the most significant performance gains.

Measure Improvement: After making code changes, profiling allows you to quantify the impact of your optimizations and ensure they're actually improving performance.
Understand Program Behavior: Profiling can provide insights into how your program actually executes, helping you identify unexpected behavior or inefficiencies.

Common Profiling Tools in Python:

cProfile: Built-in profiler that provides detailed statistics on function calls and their execution times.
line_profiler: Third-party profiler that offers line-by-line profiling, allowing you to see how much time is spent executing each line of code.
memory_profiler: Another third-party library that helps identify memory bottlenecks by tracking memory allocations throughout your program's execution.

How to Profile Your Python Code:

Choose a Profiling Tool: Select the tool that best suits your profiling needs. cProfile is a good starting point for general profiling, while line_profiler or memory_profiler can be used for more specific analysis.

Run Your Program with the Profiler: Integrate the chosen profiler into your code execution. Each profiler has its own way of achieving this, often through command-line arguments or function decorators.

Analyze the Results: The profiler will generate a report that details the collected data. This report will typically show you the functions that take the most time, the number of times they are called, and other relevant metrics.

Optimize Your Code: Based on the profiling results, identify areas for improvement. This might involve refactoring code, using more efficient algorithms, or optimizing data structures.

Re-profile and Iterate: After making code changes, re-run your program with the profiler to measure the impact of your optimizations. This iterative process helps you pinpoint and address the most critical bottlenecks in your code.

Performance Analysis Beyond Profiling:

Profiling is a powerful tool, but it's not the only aspect of performance analysis. Here are some additional considerations:

Understanding Time and Space Complexity: Analyze the theoretical time and space complexity of your algorithms. This can help you identify potential bottlenecks before you even start profiling.

Benchmarking: Compare the performance of your code with alternative approaches or libraries using benchmarking tools.

Memory Leaks: Use memory profiling tools to identify and fix memory leaks that can lead to performance degradation over time.

Conclusion:

By incorporating profiling and performance analysis into your development process, you can ensure your Python applications run efficiently and deliver a smooth user experience. Remember, profiling is an iterative process. Regularly profile your code, identify bottlenecks, optimize, and re-profile to achieve optimal performance for your Python applications.

6.1 Identifying Bottlenecks: Tools and Techniques

In the fast-paced world of software development, performance is king. Even the most well-designed application can come to a screeching halt if it's riddled with bottlenecks. Bottlenecks are sections of your code or system that significantly slow down the overall execution. Identifying and eliminating these bottlenecks is crucial for optimizing your application's performance and user experience.

Common Bottlenecks in Software:

CPU Bottlenecks: When your program requires more processing power than your CPU can provide, it can lead to slow execution and sluggish responsiveness.
Memory Bottlenecks: If your program tries to use more memory than your system has readily available, it can resort to slow disk swaps, significantly impacting performance.

I/O Bottlenecks: Operations that involve waiting for external resources like databases, network requests, or disk access can create bottlenecks if not handled efficiently.

Algorithmic Bottlenecks: Inefficient algorithms within your code can lead to excessive processing time, especially for large datasets.

Techniques for Identifying Bottlenecks:

Profiling: This is a core technique that involves measuring how your program executes. Tools like cProfile or line_profiler in Python can pinpoint functions or lines of code that take excessive time or memory.

Monitoring and Logging: Continuously monitor your application's performance metrics like CPU usage, memory consumption, and response times. Logs can provide valuable insights into potential bottlenecks, especially in production environments.

Code Reviews: Examining your code with a focus on performance can help identify areas for improvement. Look for complex algorithms, unnecessary loops, or redundant operations.

Load Testing: Simulate high user loads on your application to identify bottlenecks that might not surface during normal usage. Tools like JMeter or Locust can be used for load testing.

Optimizing Your Application:

Once you've identified bottlenecks, it's time to optimize your code:

Algorithm Replacement: Consider replacing inefficient algorithms with more optimized alternatives. Data structures can also play a role, so choose the right ones for your needs.

Code Refactoring: Restructure your code to improve readability and maintainability. This can sometimes lead to performance improvements as well.

Caching: Implement caching mechanisms to store frequently accessed data in memory, reducing the need for repeated database queries or file I/O operations.
Asynchronous Programming: For I/O bound tasks, consider using asynchronous programming techniques (like

asyncio in Python) to handle multiple requests concurrently without blocking the main thread.

Additional Considerations:

Hardware Upgrades: In some cases, a hardware upgrade (like adding more RAM or a faster CPU) might be necessary to address bottlenecks, especially for CPU or memory-bound applications.

Database Optimization: Ensure your database is properly indexed and queries are efficient. This can significantly reduce I/O wait times when fetching data.

Remember: Identifying and eliminating bottlenecks is an ongoing process. As your application grows and evolves, new bottlenecks might emerge. Regularly profiling, monitoring, and analyzing your application's performance is essential for maintaining optimal speed and efficiency.

By employing these techniques and considerations, you can become a bottleneck-hunting pro, ensuring your software applications run smoothly and deliver a fantastic user experience.

6.2 Optimizing Code for Parallel Execution

In the ever-growing world of computing, where data keeps getting bigger and tasks become more complex, squeezing the most performance out of your code is essential. One powerful approach to achieve this is by optimizing your code for parallel execution. This means structuring your code to leverage multiple processors or cores in your system, enabling them to work on different parts of the task simultaneously.

Understanding Parallel Execution:

Serial vs. Parallel Execution:
Serial execution: Tasks are executed one after another. Imagine a single waiter in a restaurant taking orders sequentially.
Parallel execution: Tasks are divided into smaller subtasks that can be executed concurrently on multiple processors. It's like having multiple waiters taking orders simultaneously, improving efficiency.

Benefits of Parallel Execution:

Reduced Execution Time: By distributing the workload across multiple processors, the overall execution time of your program can be significantly reduced, especially for tasks that can be easily broken down into independent subtasks. Improved Scalability: As hardware continues to evolve with increasing core counts, code optimized for parallel execution is well-positioned to take advantage of these advancements.

Challenges of Parallel Execution:

Data Dependencies: Not all parts of your code can be executed in parallel. If tasks have dependencies on the results of other tasks, they need to be executed in a specific order.

Communication Overhead: Coordinating and communicating between parallel tasks can introduce some overhead, which needs to be balanced against the gains from parallelization.

Optimizing Code for Parallel Execution:

Identifying Parallelism Opportunities: Analyze your code to find sections that can be broken down into independent subtasks. Look for loops, calculations, or data processing operations that can be performed concurrently.

Parallelization Techniques:

Loop parallelization: Utilize libraries or compiler directives to distribute loop iterations across multiple processors.

Task-based parallelism: Break down your program into smaller, independent tasks that can be executed concurrently using frameworks like OpenMP or Threading libraries.

Divide-and-conquer algorithms: Design algorithms that work by recursively dividing a problem into smaller subproblems, allowing for parallel execution of the subproblems.

Data Sharing and Synchronization: When multiple tasks need to access or modify shared data, proper synchronization mechanisms like locks or semaphores are crucial to avoid data races and ensure consistent results.

Libraries and Frameworks for Parallel Programming:

OpenMP: A popular set of compiler directives for shared-memory multiprocessing programming, allowing for parallel execution of loops and code sections.

Threading Libraries: Python's threading module or C++'s std::thread library provide functionalities for creating and managing threads for parallel execution.

Higher-level Frameworks: Libraries like NumPy or libraries built on top of MPI (Message Passing Interface) can simplify parallel programming for specific tasks like scientific computing or distributed processing.

Considerations for Effective Parallelization:

Amdahl's Law: This law states that the theoretical speedup achieved through parallelization is limited by the sequential portion of your code. Not all code can be parallelized, so focus on sections that offer significant gains.

Overhead vs. Benefit: The communication and synchronization overhead introduced by parallelization should be outweighed by the actual speedup achieved.

Conclusion:

Optimizing code for parallel execution requires careful analysis, strategic planning, and the use of appropriate tools and libraries. By effectively leveraging parallelism, you can unlock significant performance improvements in your computationally intensive applications, making them faster and more efficient. Remember, successful parallelization is an ongoing process. As your code evolves, you might need to revisit and refine your parallelization strategies to maintain optimal performance.

6.3 Memory Management and Thread/Process Overhead

In the realm of programming, memory management and thread/process overhead are fundamental concepts that impact application performance and resource utilization. Here's a breakdown of these concepts and how they interplay:

Memory Management:

Process vs. Thread Memory:

Processes: Each process has its own virtual address space and manages its own memory allocation and deallocation. This isolation ensures processes don't interfere with each other's memory usage.

.

Threads: Threads within a process share the same address space. They can access and modify memory allocated to the process, but each thread typically has its own private stack space for local variables and function calls.

Memory Allocation and Deallocation: Efficient memory management involves allocating memory only when needed and deallocating it promptly when it's no longer in use. Memory leaks, where memory is allocated but not released, can lead to performance degradation over time.

Memory Management Techniques: Programming languages often provide features like garbage collection (automatic memory management) or manual memory management with functions like malloc and free (C) to allocate and deallocate memory.

Thread/Process Overhead:

Process Creation: Creating a new process is a relatively expensive operation compared to creating a thread. This is because the operating system needs to allocate memory for the new process's address space, copy necessary resources from the parent process, and set up the process control block.

Thread Creation: Creating a new thread within a process is generally less expensive than creating a new process. Threads share the process's address space, so there's no need for separate memory allocation. However, the operating system still needs to set up some thread-specific data structures.

Context Switching: When the CPU switches between processes or threads, it needs to save the state of the current process/thread (registers, program counter) and load the state of the new one. This context switching can introduce overhead, especially for frequent switching.

The Trade-Off:

The choice between using processes or threads depends on the nature of your application:

Processes: Suitable for isolating tasks that don't share data or require independent memory management. Useful for long-running tasks or tasks that can potentially crash without affecting the entire application.

Threads: Ideal for tasks that need to share data frequently or cooperate closely. They can improve performance for CPU-bound tasks by utilizing multiple cores. However, excessive thread creation and context switching can lead to overhead.

Memory Management and Thread/Process Overhead: The Interplay

Thread Safety: When multiple threads access shared memory, proper synchronization mechanisms like locks or mutexes are crucial to prevent data races and ensure data consistency. This synchronization can introduce some overhead, but it's essential for thread safety.

Memory Leaks in Threads: Memory leaks within threads can be just as detrimental as in processes. Since threads share the process's address space, a leak in one thread can impact the entire process's memory usage.

Optimizing Performance:

Memory Management: Adopt best practices for memory management in your code. Use appropriate data structures, avoid unnecessary copying, and properly deallocate memory when it's no longer needed.

Thread Usage: Carefully consider the need for threads. If tasks are truly independent, processes might be a better choice. For CPU-bound tasks with frequent data sharing, threads can improve performance. However, limit excessive thread creation and manage synchronization effectively.

Conclusion:

Understanding memory management and thread/process overhead is essential for writing efficient and performant applications. By carefully selecting between processes and threads, managing memory effectively, and minimizing overhead, you can create applications that utilize system resources efficiently and deliver a smooth user experience.

6.4 Case Study: Performance Optimization of a Multithreaded Application

Scenario: Imagine a multithreaded application that processes large image files concurrently using multiple threads. Each thread loads an image, applies various filters, and saves the processed image. Initially, the application exhibits slow performance and doesn't fully utilize the available CPU cores.

Profiling and Bottleneck Identification:

Profiling: We use a profiling tool like cProfile or line_profiler to analyze the application's performance.

Bottleneck Discovery: Profiling reveals that a significant portion of time is spent on loading images from disk, which is an I/O bound operation. This indicates an I/O bottleneck.

Optimization Strategies:

Minimize I/O Operations: Analyze the image processing logic to see if any filter operations can be optimized to reduce the number of times the image data needs to be loaded from disk.

Thread Pooling: Implement a thread pool to manage a fixed number of worker threads. This avoids the overhead of creating and destroying threads for each image.

Disk Caching: Consider using a disk caching mechanism to store frequently accessed images in memory, reducing the need for repeated disk reads.

Implementation:

Thread Pool: We modify the application to use a thread pool with a limited number of worker threads. The main thread reads images from a queue and assigns them to available worker threads.

Python
```python
from concurrent.futures import ThreadPoolExecutor

# Define image processing function
def process_image(image_path):
  # Load image, apply filters, save processed image
  ...
```

```
# Create a thread pool with 4 worker threads
executor = ThreadPoolExecutor(max_workers=4)

# Main thread loop
while True:
  image_path = get_next_image_path()
  if not image_path:
    break
  future = executor.submit(process_image, image_path)
  # .. do other work while images are processed concurrently
Use code with caution.
content_copy
```

Disk Caching (Optional): If the application frequently processes the same images, explore using a library like filecache to cache them in memory. This can significantly reduce disk access times.

Re-profiling and Evaluation:

Re-run profiler: After implementing the optimizations, we re-profile the application to measure the impact.
Performance Improvement: Ideally, the profiling results should show a decrease in the time spent on I/O operations

and an increase in CPU utilization, indicating improved performance.

Additional Considerations:

Fine-tuning Thread Pool Size: The optimal number of threads in the pool depends on factors like the number of CPU cores, I/O wait times, and the amount of processing required per image. Experiment with different thread pool sizes to find the best balance.

Synchronization: If image processing involves modifying shared resources, ensure proper synchronization mechanisms are in place to prevent race conditions.

Deadlocks: Avoid scenarios where threads wait for each other indefinitely, leading to deadlocks. This can happen with improper use of locks or other synchronization primitives.

Conclusion:

This case study demonstrates how profiling and bottleneck identification can lead to targeted optimizations in a multithreaded application. By addressing I/O bottlenecks and implementing thread pooling, we can improve the application's performance and resource utilization. Remember that performance optimization is an iterative process. Continuously profile, analyze, and refine your application to ensure it delivers optimal performance under various workloads.

Chapter 7

Building Scalable and Responsive Architectures

In today's digital landscape, applications are expected to be not only functional but also adaptable and resilient. They need to handle growing user bases, increased traffic, and ever-evolving requirements. This is where scalable and responsive architectures come into play. These architectures are designed to gracefully adapt to changing demands while delivering a smooth user experience.

Core Principles of Scalable and Responsive Architectures:

Modular Design: Break down your application into smaller, independent, and well-defined modules with clear interfaces. This modularity promotes loose coupling, making it easier to scale individual modules without affecting the entire system.

Separation of Concerns: Separate the application logic from infrastructure concerns. This allows you to choose the most

appropriate technology stack for each layer (e.g., database, web server) and independently scale them based on their specific needs.

Distributed Systems: Consider distributing your application across multiple servers or cloud instances. This allows for horizontal scaling by adding more resources (servers) as traffic increases.

Load Balancing: Distribute incoming traffic across multiple servers to prevent overloading any single server and ensure smooth performance under heavy loads.

Asynchronous Programming: Techniques like asyncio in Python or coroutines in Go can improve responsiveness by handling multiple requests concurrently without blocking the main thread. This is particularly beneficial for I/O bound operations like network requests or database interactions.

Caching: Implement caching mechanisms at different layers (client-side, server-side) to store frequently accessed data. This reduces the load on your backend services and improves response times for users.

API Design: If your application involves microservices, design well-documented and efficient APIs for communication between services. This promotes loose coupling and facilitates independent scaling of individual services.

Benefits of Scalable and Responsive Architectures:

Improved Performance: By handling increased traffic efficiently, these architectures ensure a smooth user experience even under load.

High Availability: Distributed systems and redundancy can minimize downtime and improve the application's fault tolerance.

Flexibility and Maintainability: Modular design and separation of concerns make it easier to adapt the application to changing requirements and integrate new features.

Cost-Effectiveness: You can scale resources up or down based on actual usage, potentially leading to cost savings on infrastructure.

Making the Right Choices:

The optimal architecture for your application depends on several factors:

Application Type: Web applications, mobile apps, or real-time chat applications will have different scaling needs. Expected Traffic Volume: If you anticipate a rapidly growing user base, a distributed architecture might be necessary from the start.

Complexity: For simpler applications, a monolithic architecture might be sufficient initially, but consider scalability as your application evolves.

Tools and Technologies:

Cloud Platforms: Cloud platforms like AWS, Azure, or GCP offer on-demand resources and managed services that can simplify building and scaling applications.

Microservices Frameworks: Frameworks like Spring Boot (Java) or NestJS (JavaScript) can help structure your application as a collection of loosely coupled microservices.

Containerization Technologies: Docker containers offer a lightweight way to package and deploy your application code, making it easier to manage and scale across different environments.

Remember: Building scalable and responsive architectures is an ongoing process. Continuously monitor your application's performance, identify bottlenecks, and adapt your architecture as your needs evolve. By following these principles and leveraging the available tools and technologies, you can create applications that can handle ever-increasing demands and deliver a consistently positive user experience.

7.1 Designing for Concurrency: Patterns and Frameworks

In the realm of software development, concurrency is a fundamental concept that allows applications to handle multiple tasks simultaneously. This can significantly improve responsiveness and performance, especially for tasks that don't require strict sequential execution. However, designing concurrent applications can be challenging due to the potential for race conditions and other synchronization issues. Here, we'll delve into design patterns and frameworks that can help you navigate the world of concurrent programming.

Common Concurrency Patterns:

Producer-Consumer: This pattern involves two entities: a producer that generates data and a consumer that processes it. A buffer is used to decouple the producer and consumer, allowing them to operate at different speeds. This pattern is useful for tasks like buffering network requests or processing data streams.

Thread Pool: This pattern utilizes a fixed-size pool of threads to handle incoming tasks. Tasks are submitted to a queue, and available threads from the pool pick up and execute them. This helps manage the number of concurrent threads and reduces the overhead of creating and destroying threads for each task.

Monitor/Wait: This pattern involves a shared state object (monitor) and two operations: wait and notify. Threads can wait on the monitor until a specific condition is met, and notify can be used to signal waiting threads when the condition changes. This pattern helps synchronize access to shared resources and prevent race conditions.

Active Object: This pattern encapsulates task execution within an object. Tasks are submitted to the active object, which maintains its own thread and manages the execution of submitted tasks. This pattern promotes encapsulation and simplifies concurrent programming.

Popular Concurrency Frameworks:

Java:

java.util.concurrent package: Provides a rich set of classes for concurrency including thread pools, executors, locks, and semaphores.

Fork/Join Framework: A higher-level framework for parallel execution of divide-and-conquer algorithms.

Python:

threading module: Offers basic functionalities for creating and managing threads.

asyncio library: Enables asynchronous programming for non-blocking I/O operations, improving responsiveness in I/O bound applications.

Go:

Go routines (goroutines): Lightweight threads built into the Go language that make concurrency a core feature.
Channels: A communication mechanism for goroutines to synchronize and exchange data.

Choosing the Right Pattern or Framework:

The selection of a pattern or framework depends on the specific needs of your application:

Complexity: For simpler concurrency needs, the built-in libraries (threading in Python, java.util.concurrent in Java) might suffice.

Task Type: If your application involves asynchronous I/O operations, asyncio in Python or Go routines with channels can be a good fit.

Synchronization Requirements: For complex synchronization scenarios, patterns like Monitor/Wait or higher-level frameworks like Fork/Join can provide robust solutions.

Additional Considerations:

Error Handling: Concurrency introduces new challenges in error handling. Design your code to handle exceptions and potential race conditions effectively.

Testing: Thoroughly test your concurrent code to identify and eliminate race conditions and deadlocks. Unit tests and integration tests are crucial for ensuring the correctness of your concurrent applications.

Performance: While concurrency can improve performance, it's not a silver bullet. Over-concurrency can lead to overhead and context switching issues. Profile your application to identify bottlenecks and optimize accordingly.

Conclusion:

Design patterns and frameworks offer valuable tools for building robust and efficient concurrent applications. By understanding these patterns, selecting the appropriate framework for your language, and following best practices, you can harness the power of concurrency to create applications that are responsive, scalable, and performant under load. Remember, concurrency is a powerful tool, but it requires careful consideration and skillful implementation to reap its full benefits.

.7.2 Fault Tolerance and Error Handling in Concurrent Systems

In the fast-paced world of concurrent programming, where multiple tasks execute simultaneously, ensuring smooth operation and handling unexpected issues becomes paramount. This is where tolerance and error handling come into play. They are crucial for building resilient concurrent systems that can gracefully handle failures and maintain functionality.

Understanding Errors in Concurrent Systems:

Race Conditions: When multiple threads access shared data without proper synchronization, it can lead to race conditions. The outcome depends on the unpredictable timing of thread execution, potentially resulting in incorrect data or program crashes.

Deadlocks: A deadlock occurs when two or more threads are waiting for each other to release resources, creating a permanent state of waiting with no progress.
Resource Exhaustion: If threads create too many resources (like files or network connections) without proper management, it can lead to resource exhaustion and system failures.

External Errors: Even well-designed systems can encounter external errors like network outages or hardware failures.
Tolerance and Error Handling Techniques:

Defensive Programming: Write code that anticipates potential errors and includes checks to validate data and handle unexpected conditions.

Timeouts: Set timeouts for operations to prevent threads from waiting indefinitely for resources or responses.

Retries: Implement retry logic with exponential backoff for handling transient errors like network timeouts. This allows the system to automatically retry the operation after a short delay.

Exception Handling: Utilize exception handling mechanisms provided by your programming language to catch errors and take appropriate actions like logging, retrying, or gracefully failing the operation.

Resource Management: Carefully manage resources like locks, files, and network connections to avoid leaks and deadlocks. Use techniques like RAII (Resource Acquisition Is Initialization) in C++ or with statements in Python to ensure proper resource cleanup.

Monitoring and Logging: Continuously monitor your concurrent system for errors and performance issues. Implement robust logging to capture error details and facilitate troubleshooting.

Designing for Tolerance:

Thread Safety: When multiple threads access shared data, ensure proper synchronization mechanisms like locks or semaphores are in place to prevent race conditions.

Redundancy: Consider implementing redundant components or failover mechanisms for critical parts of your system. This can improve fault tolerance by allowing the system to continue operating even if some components fail.

Testing for Concurrency Issues:

Unit Tests: Although traditional unit tests can be helpful, they might not be sufficient for uncovering concurrency issues.

Concurrent Unit Testing Frameworks: Utilize frameworks specifically designed for testing concurrent code. These frameworks allow you to simulate multiple threads and test for race conditions and deadlocks.

Stress Testing: Subject your concurrent system to high loads to identify bottlenecks and potential failure points under stress.

Benefits of Effective Tolerance and Error Handling:

Improved System Reliability: By gracefully handling errors and recovering from failures, you create a more reliable system that can withstand unexpected situations.

Reduced Downtime: Effective error handling minimizes system downtime and ensures users experience minimal disruption when errors occur.

Enhanced Maintainability: Well-structured error handling with proper logging makes it easier to identify and debug issues in your concurrent system.

Conclusion:

Tolerance and error handling are essential aspects of building robust and resilient concurrent systems. By employing these techniques, designing for thread safety, and utilizing appropriate testing strategies, you can create concurrent applications that are reliable, performant, and can handle the inevitable errors and challenges that arise in real-world scenarios. Remember, a well-designed concurrent system should not just be fast, but also able to gracefully handle the bumps along the road.

7.3 Load Balancing and Distributed Processing Strategies

In the realm of computing, where data keeps growing and demands keep rising, efficiently managing workloads is crucial. Here's a breakdown of two key strategies for achieving this: load balancing and distributed processing.

Load Balancing:

Distribution of Work: Load balancing distributes incoming requests or tasks across a pool of resources (servers, machines) to ensure no single resource is overloaded. This optimizes performance and improves responsiveness for users.

Benefits:

Scalability: As workload increases, you can add more resources to the pool, allowing the system to handle the extra load efficiently.
High Availability: If a server in the pool fails, the load balancer automatically redirects traffic to remaining servers, minimizing downtime.
Improved Performance: By distributing workload, you avoid bottlenecks on individual servers, leading to faster processing times.

Load Balancing Techniques:

DNS-based Load Balancing: Distributes traffic by manipulating Domain Name System (DNS) records to direct users to different servers based on pre-defined criteria.
Hardware Load Balancers: Dedicated hardware devices route traffic across servers based on factors like load, availability, and health checks.
Software Load Balancers: Software applications running on servers can perform load balancing tasks, offering flexibility and customization.

Distributed Processing:

Dividing and Conquering: Distributed processing breaks down large tasks into smaller subtasks that can be executed concurrently on multiple computers or cores within a system. This approach leverages the combined processing power of multiple resources to complete the task faster.

Benefits:

Faster Processing: By dividing the workload, tasks are completed in parallel, significantly reducing overall processing time.

Scalability: Similar to load balancing, distributed processing allows you to add more processing power by including additional machines in the distributed system.
Handling Large Datasets: Distributed processing is ideal for handling massive datasets that wouldn't be feasible to process on a single machine.

Distributed Processing Paradigms:

Master-Worker Model: A central coordinator (master) distributes subtasks to worker nodes, collects results, and manages the overall workflow.
MapReduce: A programming model for processing large datasets on clusters of computers. It involves a "map" phase that transforms data and a "reduce" phase that summarizes the transformed data.

Choosing the Right Strategy:

The choice between load balancing and distributed processing depends on the nature of your workload:

Load Balancing: Ideal for scenarios involving independent tasks or requests that don't require complex data exchange between them. It's commonly used for web servers, application servers, and database servers.

Distributed Processing: Suited for computationally intensive tasks that can be broken down into smaller, independent subtasks. It's often used for scientific computing, big data processing, and machine learning.

Complementary Approaches:

Load balancing and distributed processing can be used together for even greater efficiency. For instance, a distributed processing system might utilize load balancing to distribute subtasks across multiple worker nodes within the cluster.

Considerations for Both Strategies:

Network Communication: Communication overhead between resources (servers, machines) is a factor to consider. Excessive communication can negate the benefits of both approaches.

Complexity: Implementing and managing distributed systems can be more complex compared to standalone systems.

Single Point of Failure: While load balancing can improve availability, a single point of failure might exist in the load balancer itself. Similarly, in distributed processing, a failure in the master node can disrupt the entire workflow.

Conclusion:

Load balancing and distributed processing are powerful tools for managing workloads and achieving high performance in modern computing systems. Understanding the benefits and drawbacks of each approach, along with the considerations for implementation, allows you to choose the right strategy or a combination of both to meet the specific needs of your application. By effectively distributing workload and leveraging the combined power of multiple resources, you can create efficient and scalable systems that can handle even the most demanding tasks.

7.4 Case Study: Scalable Data Processing Pipeline with Parallelism

Scenario: Imagine a company that analyzes large datasets containing customer purchase history. Their existing data processing pipeline struggles to handle the growing data volume, leading to long processing times and hindering valuable business insights.

Challenges:

Slow Processing: The current pipeline processes data sequentially, resulting in bottlenecks and extended processing times.
Limited Scalability: The pipeline can't handle increasing data volumes without significant infrastructure upgrades.
Missed Opportunities: Delays in data processing prevent the company from capitalizing on real-time insights for targeted marketing campaigns or inventory management.

Proposed Solution: Parallel Data Processing Pipeline

We propose a revamped data processing pipeline that leverages parallelism to improve performance and scalability:

Data Preprocessing: The incoming data stream is first divided into smaller chunks.

Parallelization: Each data chunk is processed concurrently on multiple computing resources using a distributed processing framework like Apache Spark.

Data Transformation and Analysis: Each processing unit performs the necessary data cleaning, transformation, and analysis tasks on its assigned chunk.

Aggregation and Reporting: The results from each processing unit are aggregated, and final reports are generated.

Benefits of Parallel Processing:

Faster Processing: By distributing the workload across multiple resources, the overall processing time is significantly reduced.

Improved Scalability: The pipeline can easily scale to handle larger datasets by adding more processing units to the distributed system.

Real-time Insights: Faster processing allows for near real-time data analysis, enabling quicker decision-making based on the latest data.

Implementation with Apache Spark:

Apache Spark is a popular open-source framework well-suited for large-scale data processing. It provides APIs for:

Resilient Distributed Datasets (RDDs): A fault-tolerant data structure that can be distributed across a cluster of machines.
Transformations: Functions to manipulate and analyze data within RDDs.
Actions: Operations to trigger computations and generate results from RDDs.

Spark Job Example:

```python
Python
from pyspark.sql import SparkSession

spark = SparkSession.builder.appName("Scalable Data Processing").getOrCreate()

# Read data from a file
data = spark.read.csv("data.csv")
```

```
# Split data into chunks (RDDs)
data_chunks = data.rdd.repartition(4)

# Define a transformation function for data cleaning and
analysis
def process_chunk(chunk):
  # ... data cleaning and analysis logic
  return processed_data

# Apply the transformation function to each chunk in
parallel
processed_data = data_chunks.map(process_chunk)

# Combine results and generate final report
# ...

# Stop the Spark session
spark.stop()
```

Use code with caution.

content_copy

Additional Considerations:

Monitoring and Optimization: Continuously monitor the performance of the pipeline and identify potential bottlenecks. Optimize the code and resource allocation for better efficiency.

Error Handling: Implement robust error handling techniques to ensure the pipeline gracefully handles failures and data inconsistencies.

Cost Optimization: Explore cost-effective cloud-based solutions for running the distributed processing framework.

Conclusion:

By adopting a parallel data processing pipeline with a framework like Apache Spark, the company can achieve significant improvements in performance and scalability. This enables them to process large datasets faster, gain real-time insights from their data, and make data-driven decisions that can lead to a competitive advantage. Remember, this is a simplified example, and real-world implementations might involve more complex data transformations and aggregations.

Chapter 8
Advanced Topics in Parallel Programming

As we delve deeper into the world of parallel programming, we encounter a vast array of advanced topics that push the boundaries of performance and efficiency. Here, we'll explore some of these concepts to broaden your understanding of concurrent and parallel programming:

Memory Consistency Models:

Traditional vs. Relaxed Models:

Traditional models (Sequential Consistency) guarantee that all processors see memory updates in the same order they were issued. This simplifies reasoning about concurrent code but can introduce overhead.

Relaxed models (e.g., Weak Consistency) allow for more optimizations by relaxing the ordering guarantees. This can improve performance but requires careful consideration of potential race conditions.

Understanding the memory consistency model used by your programming language or hardware is crucial for writing correct and efficient parallel programs.

Advanced Synchronization Techniques:

Beyond Locks: While locks (mutexes) are a fundamental tool for synchronization, they can create bottlenecks. Techniques like lock-free data structures and optimistic concurrency control can improve performance in specific scenarios.

CAS (Compare-And-Swap): An atomic instruction that allows a thread to compare a value in memory with an expected value and, if they match, update the memory location with a new value. This can be used to implement lock-free data structures.

Parallel Algorithms:

Beyond Loop Parallelization: While loop parallelization is a common technique, exploring advanced algorithms designed for parallel execution can unlock further performance gains. Examples include parallel sorting algorithms (e.g., Merge Sort) or parallel graph algorithms (e.g., PageRank).

Algorithmic Skew: Be aware of potential algorithmic skew, where tasks within a parallel algorithm have significantly different execution times. This can lead to load imbalances and hinder overall performance.

Heterogeneous Parallel Computing:

Beyond CPUs: Modern systems often have a mix of processing units like CPUs, GPUs (Graphics Processing Units), and FPGAs (Field-Programmable Gate Arrays). Utilizing these diverse resources effectively requires specialized programming models and tools.

OpenCL and CUDA: Programming languages like OpenCL and CUDA allow programmers to target heterogeneous systems and leverage the parallel processing power of GPUs for specific tasks.

Formal Verification of Concurrent Programs:

Reasoning about Concurrency: Verifying the correctness of concurrent programs can be challenging due to the potential for race conditions and other synchronization issues. Formal verification techniques utilize mathematical methods to prove the absence of errors in concurrent code.

Static and Dynamic Analysis Tools: Static analysis tools can identify potential concurrency issues in code without actually running it. Dynamic analysis tools can monitor program execution and detect race conditions at runtime.

Challenges and Considerations:

Increased Complexity: Advanced parallel programming techniques often come with increased complexity. Carefully evaluate the trade-off between performance gains and the added complexity of implementing and maintaining the code.

Debugging: Debugging concurrent programs can be more challenging than debugging sequential programs. Utilize debugging tools and techniques specifically designed for concurrent systems.

Conclusion:

The realm of advanced parallel programming offers a rich set of concepts and techniques to explore. By understanding memory consistency models, advanced synchronization, parallel algorithms, heterogeneous computing, and formal verification, you can unlock the full potential of parallel programming. However, remember to carefully consider the complexity involved and choose the appropriate techniques based on the specific needs of your application. As hardware continues to evolve with more complex architectures, the importance of mastering these advanced topics will only grow in the future.

8.1 Parallel Scientific Computing with Libraries like NumPy

NumPy, a fundamental library for scientific computing in Python, offers capabilities beyond efficient array manipulation. It provides a foundation for parallel computing, allowing you to leverage multiple cores or processors to accelerate computationally intensive tasks. Here's how NumPy empowers parallel scientific computing:

Vectorization:

Core Principle: NumPy operations are vectorized, meaning they operate on entire arrays simultaneously instead of iterating through elements one by one. This inherent parallelism translates to significant performance gains for calculations involving large datasets.

Python
import numpy as np

```
# Sequential summation (slow)
total_sum = 0
for i in range(1000000):
  total_sum += i

# Vectorized summation (fast)
large_array = np.arange(1000000)
vectorized_sum = np.sum(large_array)
```
Use code with caution.
content_copy

Multiprocessing with multiprocessing Module:

Leveraging Multiple Cores: The multiprocessing module in Python, often used in conjunction with NumPy, enables you to distribute tasks across multiple CPU cores within a single machine. This approach is ideal for problems that can be broken down into independent subtasks.

Python
```
from multiprocessing import Pool

def compute_intensive_task(data_chunk):
  # Perform calculations on a chunk of data
  return processed_data

# Split data into chunks
data_chunks = np.array_split(large_array, num_cores)

# Create a pool of worker processes
with Pool(processes=num_cores) as pool:
  # Apply the function to each chunk in parallel
  results = pool.map(compute_intensive_task, data_chunks)

# Combine the results
final_result = np.concatenate(results)
```
Use code with caution.

content_copy

Distributed Computing with Libraries like Dask:

Scaling Beyond a Single Machine: For truly large-scale problems, libraries like Dask extend NumPy's capabilities to distributed computing environments. Dask creates parallel NumPy-like arrays and dataframes that can span multiple machines in a cluster. This allows you to harness the combined processing power of a distributed system for massive datasets.

Python
import dask.array as da

# Create a Dask array distributed across a cluster
distributed_array = da.from_array(large_array, chunks=(chunk_size,))

# Perform computations on the distributed array
processed_array = distributed_array * 2   # Element-wise multiplication

# Trigger computation and get results
result = processed_array.compute()
Use code with caution.
content_copy

.

Choosing the Right Approach:

Problem Size and Complexity: The choice between vectorization, multiprocessing, or distributed computing depends on the size and nature of your problem. For smaller datasets, vectorization might suffice. For problems with independent subtasks, multiprocessing can be effective. Distributed computing becomes necessary for extremely large datasets that require the combined power of multiple machines.

Benefits of Parallel Scientific Computing:

Faster Execution Times: By utilizing multiple cores or processors, parallel computing significantly reduces the time it takes to complete complex calculations.
Handling Larger Datasets: Parallel approaches enable you to tackle problems involving massive datasets that wouldn't be feasible on a single machine.
Improved Scalability: As your computational needs grow, you can easily scale your parallel computing environment by adding more cores or machines to the cluster.

Considerations and Challenges:

Overhead: Introducing parallelism can introduce some overhead for task creation and communication between processes. Ensure the benefits outweigh the overhead for your specific use case.

Algorithmic Suitability: Not all scientific computing problems are inherently parallelizable. Analyze your algorithms to identify opportunities for parallelization.

Debugging: Debugging parallel code can be more complex than debugging sequential code. Utilize debugging tools and techniques specifically designed for concurrent systems.

Conclusion:

NumPy, along with other libraries and tools, empowers you to leverage the power of parallel computing for scientific applications. By understanding vectorization, multiprocessing, and distributed computing, and carefully considering the trade-offs involved, you can significantly accelerate your scientific computations and unlock new possibilities for data analysis and modeling. Remember, parallel computing is a powerful tool, but it requires careful planning and implementation to achieve optimal performance and efficiency.

8.2 GPU Programming with Libraries like PyTorch and TensorFlow

In the realm of deep learning, processing massive datasets and complex neural network architectures can be computationally expensive. This is where Graphics Processing Units (GPUs) come into play. GPUs excel at parallel processing, making them ideal for accelerating deep learning workloads. Frameworks like PyTorch and TensorFlow offer functionalities to leverage GPUs for efficient deep learning training and inference.

Why GPUs for Deep Learning?

Massive Parallelism: GPUs are designed with thousands of cores compared to a CPU's limited cores. This allows them to handle many computations simultaneously, significantly speeding up matrix multiplications, a fundamental operation in deep learning.

High Memory Bandwidth: GPUs have wider memory bandwidth compared to CPUs, enabling faster access to large datasets required for training deep learning models.

Deep Learning Frameworks with GPU Support:

PyTorch and TensorFlow: Both PyTorch and TensorFlow provide comprehensive libraries for building, training, and deploying deep learning models. They offer functionalities to seamlessly utilize GPUs for these tasks.

Key Concepts:

CUDA: CUDA (Compute Unified Device Architecture) is a parallel computing platform developed by Nvidia for programming GPUs. While not strictly required for using PyTorch or TensorFlow with GPUs, understanding CUDA can provide finer-grained control over GPU operations.

Tensor Cores: Modern GPUs include specialized Tensor Cores designed to accelerate specific operations crucial for deep learning, such as matrix multiplications. PyTorch and TensorFlow can leverage these cores for further performance gains.

Using GPUs with PyTorch and TensorFlow:

Device Selection: Both frameworks allow you to explicitly specify whether to use the CPU or GPU for computations. This can be done through function calls or context managers.

Python
# PyTorch example
device = torch.device("cuda" if torch.cuda.is_available() else "cpu")
model = MyModel().to(device)

TensorFlow example
with tf.device("/GPU:0"):
  # Define and train your model here
Use code with caution.
content_copy

Data Transfer: Datasets and model parameters need to be transferred between CPU and GPU memory for processing. Both frameworks handle these transfers automatically, but optimizing data loaders and model sizes can improve efficiency.

Benefits of GPU Programming for Deep Learning:

Faster Training Times: Training deep learning models on GPUs can significantly reduce training times, allowing for quicker experimentation and model iteration.

Handling Larger Models and Datasets: GPUs enable you to train more complex models with deeper architectures and larger datasets, leading to potentially better performance on tasks like image recognition or natural language processing.

Challenges and Considerations:

Hardware Requirements: Utilizing GPUs requires compatible hardware with sufficient memory and computational power. This can add to the cost of deep learning development and deployment.

Code Complexity: While frameworks handle most of the complexities, understanding GPU programming concepts like memory management can be beneficial for advanced users.

Not a Silver Bullet: While GPUs offer significant speedups, they might not be suitable for all deep learning tasks. Carefully evaluate your specific use case and hardware limitations before solely relying on GPUs.

Conclusion:

PyTorch and TensorFlow provide powerful tools for leveraging GPUs in deep learning. By understanding the advantages of GPUs, the core concepts involved, and the considerations for implementation, you can harness the power of GPU programming to accelerate your deep learning projects and achieve superior results. Remember, GPU programming is a valuable skill for deep learning practitioners, but it's important to use it strategically to maximize its benefits for your specific needs.

8.3 Parallel Data Processing with Frameworks like Dask

In the big data era, traditional sequential processing often struggles to handle massive datasets. This is where parallel data processing frameworks like Dask come into play. Dask empowers you to distribute data processing tasks across multiple cores or even entire clusters, significantly accelerating your computations.

Core Concepts of Dask:

Familiar API: Dask builds upon familiar libraries like NumPy and Pandas, providing parallel equivalents for their functionalities. This allows you to leverage your existing data science skills with minimal adaptation.

Task Scheduling: Dask takes your data processing workflow and breaks it down into smaller, independent tasks. These tasks are then efficiently scheduled and executed across available computing resources.

Resilience: Dask is designed to be fault-tolerant. If a worker process fails, Dask can automatically reschedule the tasks on another available resource, minimizing disruptions.
Benefits of Using Dask for Parallel Data Processing:

Faster Processing: By distributing tasks across multiple cores or machines, Dask significantly reduces the time it takes to process large datasets.

Scalability: Dask scales seamlessly from single-machine deployments to large clusters. You can easily add more resources as your data processing needs grow.

Flexibility: Dask works with various data formats, including CSV, Parquet, and HDF5. It can also handle different data structures like arrays and dataframes.

Common Dask Use Cases:

Large-Scale Data Cleaning and Transformation: Dask efficiently cleans and transforms large datasets in parallel, accelerating data preparation tasks.

Exploratory Data Analysis (EDA): Dask allows you to perform exploratory data analysis on massive datasets without being bottlenecked by processing limitations.

Machine Learning with Large Datasets: Dask integrates with popular machine learning libraries like scikit-learn, enabling parallel training and inference on large datasets.
Comparison to Traditional Data Processing Libraries:

NumPy and Pandas: While NumPy and Pandas offer efficient array and dataframe manipulation, they are primarily designed for single-machine use. Dask builds upon these libraries, providing parallel versions for large-scale data processing.

Spark: Spark is another popular framework for distributed data processing. Dask often offers a simpler API and lower overhead for smaller to medium-sized datasets. However, Spark might be preferable for very large datasets or complex workflows requiring custom partitioning and shuffling.

Getting Started with Dask:

Dask provides various functionalities depending on your needs:

Dask.array: A parallel NumPy array for efficient numerical computations on large datasets.

Dask.dataframe: A parallel Pandas dataframe for scalable data manipulation and analysis.

Dask.distributed: A scheduler for coordinating task execution across a cluster of machines.

Several tutorials and resources are available online to help you get started with Dask. Here are some popular options:

Dask Documentation: https://distributed.dask.org/
Dask   Tutorial:
https://domino.ai/blog/dask-step-by-step-tutorial

Conclusion:

Dask offers a powerful and user-friendly solution for parallel data processing. By leveraging its familiar API, fault tolerance, and scalability, you can streamline your big data workflows and extract valuable insights from massive datasets faster than ever before. As data sizes continue to grow, Dask is a valuable tool for data scientists and analysts to stay ahead of the curve. Remember, Dask is not a one-size-fits-all solution, but understanding its capabilities and limitations can help you determine if it's the right tool for your specific data processing needs.

8.4 Future-proofing your Code for Emerging Technologies

In the ever-evolving world of technology, future-proofing your code becomes a crucial practice. While predicting the exact future is impossible, here are some principles you can follow to write code that can adapt to emerging trends:

Focus on Well-Defined Abstractions:

Modular Design: Break down your codebase into smaller, well-defined modules with clear responsibilities. This promotes loose coupling, making it easier to modify or replace individual modules without affecting the entire system.

Separation of Concerns: Separate the core logic of your application from implementation details like data access or user interface rendering. This allows you to swap out these implementation details for new technologies without rewriting the core logic.

Embrace Interfaces and Design Patterns:

Interfaces: Define clear interfaces that outline what a module or component can do, not how it does it. This allows for implementing the same functionality using different technologies as they emerge.

Design Patterns: Utilize established design patterns that provide solutions to common software design problems. These patterns often promote loose coupling and maintainability, making your code more adaptable.

Prioritize Code Readability and Maintainability:

Clean Code Practices: Adhere to clean code principles like clear naming conventions, proper commenting, and well-formatted code. This makes your code easier to understand and modify, not just for you but also for future developers who might need to adapt it.

.

Detailed Documentation: Invest time in creating comprehensive documentation that explains the purpose of different code sections, design decisions made, and usage instructions. This documentation becomes invaluable when revisiting the codebase in the future.

Leverage Agnostic Libraries and Frameworks:

Technology-Independent Libraries: Choose libraries and frameworks that are less reliant on specific technologies and provide a more generic interface. This allows you to switch to alternative implementations if necessary.

Open Standards: Whenever possible, utilize open standards for data formats and communication protocols. Open standards are less likely to become obsolete and promote interoperability with future technologies.

Embrace Testable Code:

Unit Tests: Write unit tests that focus on the core functionality of individual modules. This isolates potential issues and ensures core functionalities remain intact even during future modifications.

Integration Tests: Complement unit tests with integration tests that verify how different modules interact with each other. This helps to identify potential issues when integrating new technologies.

Be Wary of Over-Engineering:

Balance is Key: While future-proofing is important, avoid over-engineering your code. Focus on building a clean and maintainable codebase that can be easily extended as needed. The YAGNI Principle: Follow the YAGNI principle (You Ain't Gonna Need It). Don't add features or functionalities for hypothetical future needs unless they are demonstrably required now.

Continuous Learning and Refactoring:

Stay Updated: Continuously learn about emerging technologies and trends in your field. This allows you to identify opportunities to refactor your codebase and leverage new advancements.

Refactoring: Schedule regular code reviews and refactoring sessions to improve code structure, remove technical debt, and adapt to changing requirements.

Remember, future-proofing is an ongoing process, not a one-time fix. By following these principles and staying adaptable, you can write code that remains relevant and maintainable as technology continues to evolve.

www.ingramcontent.com/pod-product-compliance
Lightning Source LLC
LaVergne TN
LVHW051336050326
832903LV00031B/3579